I would like to dedicate this book to one of my batchmates of LLB(Hon's) program of Dhaka Interntational University, Late Khan Abul Hossain who fought for the country in 1971 and Md Kabirul Hasan sir, the best teacher I have ever seen until now.

The second person (most senior) from the right is Late Khan Abul Hossain, my batchmate.

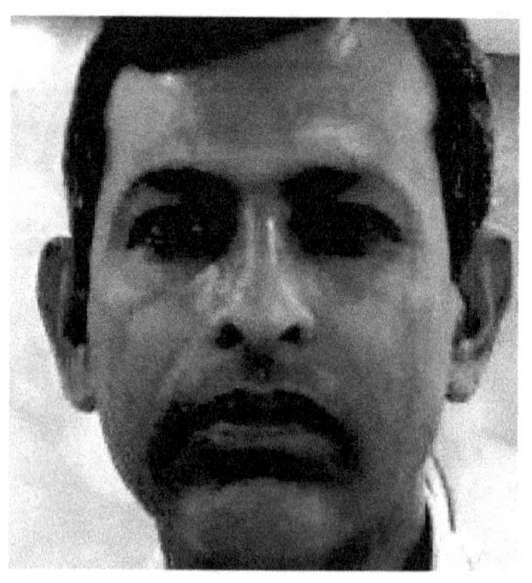

Md Kabirul Hasan sir(The photo was downloaded from his facebook, thus the resolution is quite bad)

FRAMING OF THE INCIDENTS OF INTERNATIONAL AND NATIONAL IMPORTANCE IN PRINT MEDIA OF PAKISTAN

AN EVIDENCE FROM PALWAMA ATTACK LEADING TO 27TH FEBRUARY PAK-INDIA ESCALATION AND US WITHDRAWAL FROM AFGHANISTAN

S M NAZMUZ SAKIB

Contents

Framing Of The Incidents Of International And National Importance In Print Media Of Pakistan

By
S M Nazmuz Sakib, MBA (HR), BSc (BS), Final year of LLB(Hon's).
Master of Business Administration in Human Resources,
International MBA Institute,
Samstagernstrasse 57 8832, Wollerau, Switzerland.
Bachelor of Science in Business Studies,
School of Business And Trade,
Pilatusstrasse 6003, 6003 Luzern, Switzerland.
Final Year student of Bachelor of Laws (Hon's),
Faculty of Law,
Dhaka International University,
House # 4, Road # 1, Block - F, Dhaka 1213.

About The Author

S M Nazmuz Sakib

S M Nazmuz Sakib was born in Dinajpur, Bangladesh on 16th April of 2001. He completed his Primary School Certificate (PSC) from Cotton Research Station School,

Sreepur, Gazipur; After studing several months of Class 6 in Alhaz Dhanai Bepari Memorial High School, Sreepur, Gazipur, he went to Jashore. Completed his Junior School Certificate (JSC) from Jagodishpur Mirzapur Ismail Secondary School, Jagodishour, Chaowgacha, Jashore and Secondary School Certificate (SSC) from A. K. High School And College, Dhania, Dhaka-1236. Done his Higher Secondary Certificate (HSC) from Chowgacha Government College, Chowgacha, Jashore. He completed his BSc in Business Studies gaining CGPA 4 out of 4 (1st class 1st) with 97.06% marks from School of Business and Trade, an online business school situated in Switzerland. He competed MBA in Human Resources from International MBA Institute, an online business institute in Switzerland. He is now in final year of LLB(Hon's) program of Dhaka International University, Dhaka, Bangladesh. He competed several CPD verified advanced diploma and diploma programs. Passed diploma in Human Resources (HR), Web Design, Manufacturing - Productive Management with Fundamental Tools, ISO Standards - Integrated Management System (IMS), Effective Human Resource Administration, Training of Trainers etc. and advanced diploma in Tourism and Hospitality Management, Modelling and Analytics for Supply Chain Management, Production and Operation Management, Principles of Industrial Engineering etc. He completed TESOL from Arizona State University and TEFL from Teacher Record. Passed Scrum Master Professional Certificate and got the title SMPC®. He also got Google IT Support Certificate, Google Data Analytics Certificate, IBM New Collar: Customer Engagement Specialist credential etc. Being a multidisciplinary researcher, he has 4 publications in Asian Pacific Journal of Environment and Cancer, Waste

Technology and The IUP Journal of Electrical and Electronics Engineering. Several of his article are published by Cambridge Open Engage, a publication of Cambridge University Press.

Some of the titles of his published research works are following -

1. The Impact of Oil and Gas Development on the Landscape and Surface in Nigeria

2. Assessing the Impact of Arctic Melting in the Predominantly Multilateral World System

3. LiDAR Technology-An Overview

4. Electrochemical Waste Water Treatment

Acknowledgements

All acclamation and praises are for "Almighty ALLAH". I would like to acknowledge two people. One is late Khan Abul Hossain, a Bangladeshi freedom fighter, my friend, a batchmate of mine from LLB course of Dhaka International University & with whom I spent a lot of time during my research periods. And another person is Md Kabirul Hasan sir, the best teacher of my life until today and his lectures during my preparation for Junior School Certificate (JSC) Exam was a great foundation to start my research work(s). It might be quite impossible for me to do these research(es) for human kind without their inspiration, mental support & support by giving knowledge.

Preface

This study aims to examine the framing of incidents of national and international importance in the print media of Pakistan. The study focuses on two newspapers, two events, and two time periods before and after the incidents, to analyze how the events are framed and reported by the media. The Palwama attack and US withdrawal are chosen as the events, and the study covers a period of a month and a half and two months respectively. Through content analysis of 482 articles, the study aims to conclude on the credibility of the print media in Pakistan as a source for framing incidents of national and international importance. The study will also explore the role of media as a watchdog in times of conflict and its impact on shaping public perceptions.

The study examines the framing of the Palwama incident, which led to an escalation between Pakistan and India on February 27, and the US pullout from Afghanistan in these newspapers. The study analyzes the topics, sources, and frames used by the print media in reporting these incidents, in order to evaluate the credibility of the media in framing important national and international events. The study found that the Dawn and Tribune newspapers published a significant number of articles on these events, and that they approached the events from different frames, with the Dawn focusing more on thematic framing and showing more genuine sources, while the Tribune concentrated more on its news desk. The study suggests that the media in Pakistan has the ability to diffuse tensions and promote tolerance and stability in society, and that it should self-regulate to promote peace and stability.

In summary as a poem -

Pakistan, a land of strife and turmoil,
A crucial player in the global fight
Against the terror that threatens to spoil
The peace and security of day and night.

Internal disputes and media confusion
Lead to a lack of decision-making and initiative.
Strategically relevant, fragile and fusion
Of pluralistic characteristics, a delicate initiative.

Print media, a fourth pillar of the state
Has the right to free expression, but with care
For spreading correct information to the late
For better understanding and to be aware.

The current study aims to uncover the truth
Of framing in Pakistan's print media, a proof
Of Dawn and Tribune's reporting, uncouth
Palwama incident and US pullout, aloof

The research concludes, with sources and frames
The incidents were reported, free of blames
To promote peace, stability, and refrain
From war media, and to change disputes in gains.

In conclusion, Pakistan's media must strive
To be a source of truth and hope alive.

- S M Nazmuz Sakib, the author.

CHAPTER ONE

INTRODUCTION

1.1 Background of the Study

Countries are important analytical units for the media, which shapes a country's vision and contributes to its growth as an image agent (Gartner, 1994).Countries are important analytical units for the media, which shapes a country's vision and contributes to its growth as an image agent (Gartner, 1994).Countries are important analytical units for the media, which shapes a country's vision and contributes to its growth as an image agent (Gartner, 1994).Countries are important analytical units for the media, which shapes a country's vision and contributes to its growth as an image agent (Gartner, 1994).Countries are important analytical units for the media, which shapes a country's vision and contributes to its growth as an image agent (Gartner, 1994).Countries are important analytical units for the media, which shapes a country's vision and contributes to its growth as an image agent (Gartner, 1994). According to the Pakistan Institute of Legislative Development and Transparency (2008) Pakistan has been both a victim and an ally in the worldwide war against terrorism (As of September 11th). It has had to contend with a considerable number of suicide bombs and attacks as a key target of terrorism. For decades, a large number of similar incidents have occurred at public gatherings, religious sites, and armed units, and have been documented in the media. Something fresh or significant is referred to as "news." It's a nonfiction kind of writing based on genuine occurrences. Actual event reports, on the other hand, are always appealing to the general audience. NEWS stands for North, East, West, and South, meaning that it attempts to cover news from all corners of the globe. It has become an essential and thorough source of information sharing since it answers questions like what happened, when it happened, where it happened, why it happened, who was involved, and how it happened. The news media has clearly become an essential instrument of the government in today's globalized world. It is viewed as the government's fourth estate, via which it may promote its own interests, ambitions, and purposes.

Since the beginning of the information revolution, there has been an increase in the use of news media for diverse purposes. However, it has been acknowledged as a major component in the development of opinions from its origin. The presence of a news media in a culture has a considerable impact on how the general public perceives the world. Individuals are exposed to current developments on a national and cross-border level through news media, which allows them to express their opinions (Iyengar, 1987). According to Gilboa (2006), news media is an important medium for information dissemination since it has the ability to bring to light circumstances that would otherwise go ignored. Such problems are brought to the forefront by the new media in order to place them on the priority lists of government officials and to obtain public comment on them. When it comes to getting information to in the general public and officials in a country, framing is crucial. However, because of this information flow, a number of external and internal issues develop (Shoemaker & Reese, 1996). In 1972, George Bateson proposed the concept of framing, claiming that psychological frames are a spatial limit of collaborating signals that play an important role in the setup of meta-communication (Hallahan, 2008). In the context of a story, framing is an attempt to represent the act of thinking of or explaining something new.

The action of framing is based on the establishing of an agenda, which focuses on the topic at hand. The main purpose of framing theory is to pay close attention to what happens and then attach meaning to those occurrences (Theory of Mass Communication, 2017). It is largely concerned with presenting something to a group of people. Data transmission is aided by frames, which are an abstraction of ordered messages. According to framing theory, media creates a frame by capturing and introducing items that have already been identified and contextualized. Frames are mental shortcuts that let people access the real world. Framing theory helps us to look at life and the news in a fresh light. It enables a person to evaluate what he hears, sees, or reads on television, the internet, or in print media. It allows one to make assumptions about the issues at hand and compare and contrast them in the actual world. Framing theory is multi-dimensional in and of itself, and researchers have looked at it from a variety of angles, including political, social, and communication views. Deductive generic frames are the way to go when it comes to developing comparably fresh research possibilities in this discipline. Deductive generic themes are used to indicate how media frames can be organized into predefined themes.

Now-a-days media has become an undeniable weapon of war as people have developed a concept that they will be called strong only if they remain in the warfare and if they have capacity to beat their enemy in the battlefield. However, some of the media platforms and journalists are trying to remain unbiased and present the actual picture of the specific event before people but they failed to change the mindset of large society. On the issue of Iraq, Vietnam and Afghanistan the issues were demonstrated as the War which worsen the situation most of the time. The media's position as a watchdog, monitoring and verifying the factual accuracy of the information they collect, publish, and disseminate to the public, is becoming increasingly vital, particularly during times of conflict. On the other hand, they must rely on official sources of information and are never fully free of public perceptions of what is in the national interest (Stromback and Dimitrova, 2008). The terrorist assaults on September 11th intensified a global wave of terrorism. This had a significant impact on Pakistan, which is at the forefront of the international anti-terrorism effort. After the army began a Rah-e-Nizat military attack against the South Waziristan Agency in 2009, militants penetrated North Waziristan. (Source: Javaid, 2015). Terrorist groups around the nation continued their assaults after the government and Taliban factions failed to reach an accord. Ten terrorists attacked Jinnah International Airport in Karachi, killing 36 people, including militants, and injuring 18 others (Hameed, 2015). As a result of this terrorist act, the security situation in Pakistan has deteriorated.

1.2 Media and Conflicts

"War is nothing more than ongoing politics with additional tools," stated Karl von Clausewitz, a Prussian military strategist in the 18th century. The nature of war and warfare changed as governments and societies evolved and altered. When everything is considered in context and technological development is considered, the twenty-first century's "war on terror" plainly becomes a media-led conflict (Brown and Clausewitz, 2003). Because of the government's active assistance for humanitarian catastrophes, the media affect public opinion and have a significant part in the eventual result of today's conflicts.

When it comes to the depiction of conflict, the media has the option of contributing to the escalation of tensions or remaining neutral by focusing on peaceful solutions. The role of the media in war is shaped by elements such as its ties to state or non-state players in the fight, as well as its independence from outside influences. The mainstream media is usually present when a country is actively embroiled in a crisis or conflict. The government and military exert pressure on the media to misrepresent and construct a social reality that suits their needs (Lynch, 2007), influencing and creating the media narrative of a particular battle. The New York Journal, for example, ordered Cuban Ambassador Frederick Remington to stay until the conflict began soon before the Spanish-American War of 1898. (New York Journal, WC). Hurst, r.) After noticing indicators of difficulty for a few days, Remington wrote to his supervisor, "Everything works perfectly." It's no issue. There isn't going to be a brawl. I was going to return. "Remington, Havana: Please don't go," wrote Hearst in response. I'll object, and you'll reveal the image (White,

2009). A few weeks later, an American ship sunk after exploding in Havana's harbor. The Heart's New York Journal accused the Spaniards of inexplicable happenings and initiated an intensive campaign to manipulate public opinion in favor of the war, despite the fact that the source of the deadly disaster remains unclear. The inclination of the media to argue is explained by whether or not the issue is real. A image of conflict in the Middle East, according to one research (Schinar, 2013). Asia's south-east. A similar trend may be found in the Persian Gulf, Kashmir, Chechnya, Afghanistan, Iraq, and Pakistan.

Many journalists held view that they have enough choice and eager to freely address any kind of issues as they are intelligent enough to tackle and understand any kind of issue by keeping in view the ideological limitations. Many experts, however, disagree, claiming that the ideological and organizational structure has an impact not just on journalists' everyday job routines, but also on how news organizations observe and report events. During times of conflict, for example, Herman and Chomsky (1988) accused the media of presenting any material that contradicted "official" sources as "inappropriate," thereby eliminating ideological alternatives and confining debate to the framework of political and military leaders. According to Herman and Chomsky, the media's portrayal of the Vietnam War was shaped by what remained: the antiwar movement's voices in the United States, the Vietnamese people's reasons, and the "inexpressible" sense that the United States was at war. in the same way the record of today's wars, according to Johan Galtung, a Norwegian scholar and creator of the field of peace studies, is strongly skewed in favor of war, which he labels "war journalism" (Galtung, 1998a). To underline the need of conflict reporting, Galtung invented the phrase "peace journalism." According to Galtung, the media concentrates on disputes for the sake of peace, siding with the elite while neglecting the pain of people touched by the conflict (Galtung, 1986).

According to Galtung, when it comes to documenting hostilities and fights, the media typically takes the "low route," which leads to war journalism (1998). Furthermore, it was suggested that a strategy be taken that validates the benefits of peace journalism, demotivates the war media, and concentrates on changing disputes into peaceful resolutions. War journalism, according to Galtung (1998b), is "violence-oriented, propaganda-oriented, elite-oriented, and victory-oriented." Peace journalism basically is "peace/conflict-focused, truth-focused, people-focused, and solution-focused" (Galtung. 2002a). Several media experts and professionals, on the other hand, have cast doubt on the idea of peace journalism. Hanitzsch (2007), in his studies define peace journalism a form of public relations and also it is the responsibility of the policy makers to promote peace rather than journalists as, policymakers are in charge of moving peace programmes forward. Similarly, Loyn (2007) questions the idea of peace journalism, claiming that not everyone's responsibility is to avert a war. Another perspective comes from Fawcett (2002), who held the view that the motivation of journalists to favor or oppose a certain issue or party is based on various professional and organizational reasons. According to extensive studies on conflict coverage, conventional media tends to lean more toward war aspects of the journalism rather than peace based aspect during times of conflict, intensifying the crisis and lowering the possibility of reconciliation.

Keeping in mind the above presented scenario the underlying research will propose a critical view of two key events, i.e., 27th February Pak-India oscillations and US withdrawal from Afghanistan. These incident in terms of generic frame on one hand and national and regional frames on the other hand helps us to understand how Pakistan's mainstream media i.e., Print media will highlight these issues. This study is primarily a contrast between the presentation of issues by the main framing body of the country i.e., one is Print media of the country which includes two leading newspapers i.e., Tribune and Dawn tries to find out which how these are the most credible source of information transfer and how these newspapers frame key incidents of the country and across the borders.

1.3 Important Incidents in the History of Country

Pakistan has been facing a serious issue of terrorism in almost all parts of the country and has been engaged in this war on terrorism for last many decades. For, the purpose study is investigating the unstable history of the country in the print media of Pakistan. In the way, it is engaged to analyze the 27 February Pak-India escalation and US recent withdrawal from Afghanistan. If we talk about the last two decades of Pakistan, it comes to conclusion that since 2011 it has been a victim of terrorist attacks in the form of suicide blasts, bomb explosions and rocket assaults which take the costly lives of its 15,000 security personnel and 49,000 civilizations (Raja, 2013). Moreover, in the same year Conflict Monitoring Center (2013) theorized that Pakistan has been witnessed the 376 attacks between the 9/11 and 2013 which claimed the 5,714 lives in Pakistan.

Therefore, military forces of Pakistan have been fighting with the militant groups both at inside and outside of the country for pursuit of the peace.

The section below is presented these two important incidents in the recent history which the researcher is analyzing in the Pakistan's print media by assessing the two major newspapers of the country i.e., Dawn and Tribune.

1.3.1 US Withdrawal

After the withdrawal of US and NATO troops from Afghanistan the 20-years long military campaign comes to an end in 2021. This campaign was started in 2001 aims to remove the Taliban who were providing the safe heaven to international terrorist's organizations particularly Al-Qaeda. Such removals were aimed to make the country democratically stabilized. On 31st August 2021 Taliban bring to an end the dream of making Afghanistan a democratically elected nation by firing rockets at Kabul airport as a result the final US military plane and the president of Afghanistan fled overseas, and Taliban take the control of most pf the country. The Taliban have yet to reveal the nature of their new administration or its full composition. Meanwhile, the country's humanitarian situation is rapidly deteriorating. The country is heavily reliant on foreign help, which has been banned in large part, and foreign assets have been blocked.

1.3.1.1 The US-Taliban Peace Agreement

In February 2020, a peace accord was signed among Taliban and United States which claims that the US soldiers will leave Afghanistan within 14 days. In response Taliban claimed that they will not use the land for any kind of terror activity and will not sponsor any terrorist organization including Al-Qaeda which is posing a threat to the US and its allies. At the time both parties were claiming that there will be free economic and social activities within and outside the Afghan boarders. The US also pledged to begin diplomatic dialogue with other UN Security Council members as well as Afghanistan to remove Taliban members from the UN sanctions list.

The collective agreement, which was reached without the participation of the Afghan government, also calls for the start of discussions between Afghanistan and the United States to achieve a long-term and comprehensive ceasefire. The Afghan government, for its part, has signed a joint declaration with the US endorsing these negotiations. In September 2020, inter-Afghan peace talks began in Doha, but initial expectations that these historic discussions between the Afghan government and the Taliban would bring the nation back to peace were crushed. Instead, the Taliban assaulted the Afghan government after the US declared in April 2021 that it would remove its personnel from Afghanistan by September. The Taliban managed to gain control of most of the country in just four months due to minimal opposition from government security personnel. On August 15, 2021, Afghan President Ashraf Ghani left the country when the Taliban "barely defended Kabul".

1.3.1.2 Presence and Removal of NATO and US

In 2011, in Afghanistan there reached 100,000 US troops in Afghanistan from which 14000 troops would leave the country by the end of 2018, as said by Donald Trump. On April 13, the newly appointed president Biden claim that by September 11, 2021, all US troops who were previously appointed in Afghanistan would leave the country. However, on August 31, 2021, the US military left the Afghanistan which was completely occupied by Taliban. Due to this withdrawal, there observed the deployment of 20-year US military hegemony in Afghanistan which costs more than $2 trillion. The Resolute Support Mission (RSM) which was started by NATO started leaving Afghanistan on 1st May 2021. However, 10,000 troops who were from the 36-member related to NATO and other partnered countries started deploying their troops by August 2020. In Afghanistan NATO formed RSM on the request of Afghan government the main aim of which was to assist the security forces of Afghanistan to develop a force which may be capable of defending their nation as a whole. With the introduction of RSM there observed the replacement of ISAF which deployed Afghanistan in August 2003. ISAF was led by NATO at that time. It has 130,000 troops which were from its 50-member states. In 2021 a summit was held by NATO wherein it pledged to "stand with Afghanistan, its people, and its institutions, as well as provide financial support to Afghan security forces until 2024". NATO, on the other hand, has suspended off all assistance to the Afghan government following the Taliban's control of the country.

1.3.1.3 Afghanistan's Security Situation

Afghanistan has been torn apart by war for decades, and the Global Peace Index has routinely put it among the world's least peaceful countries since 2010. In 2020, the US and the Taliban negotiated a peace accord, which has resulted in a reduction in civilian violence, with civilian deaths at their lowest level since 2012. When the peace talk starts between the Taliban and Afghan government in September 2020, during which the killings increased substantially, as both sides seek to get the upper hand through force. During the fourth quarter of 2020, there found 45 percent of increase in the civil lawsuits same as was in 2019. Khorasan which was the regional branch of the Iraq and Syria were accused due to some of the worst massacres in the region of Pakistan and Afghanistan. Mosques, squares, and even hospitals have been targeted. On August 26, 2021, the organisation claimed responsibility for a series of bombings near Kabul due to which almost 200 people were killed, including 13 US soldiers, as well as a missile attack at the airport four days later. The security situation in Afghanistan is expected to worsen further, giving a safe haven for terrorists planning new strikes in the West. 5,000 Taliban, Al-Qaeda, and Islamic State members who were imprisoned by US and NATO forces and buried at the former US facility at Bagram were released by the Taliban. The Taliban rebellion was centered in the Panjshir Valley, north of Kabul. Ahmad Masood, the son of a powerful Tajik chief who fought the Taliban in 1990 before being assassinated by al-Qaeda in 2001, rejected the Taliban and threatened to revolt. Amarullah Saleh, a former Tajik vice president, has joined the group.

1.3.1.4 Afghanistan's Economic and Humanitarian Situation

Afghanistan's gross domestic product (GDP) is estimated to account for nearly 40% of the country's GDP by 2020 in terms of costs and economic implications for "managing, preventing, and coping with the effects of violence." I believe this is the case. With 90% of the population surviving on less than $2 a day, the economy is built on handouts. Most help and financial reserves were withdrawn when the Taliban took power, bringing Afghanistan to the verge of economic ruin. The impacts of the Covid-19 crisis have already had an impact on the economy, with real GDP estimated to shrink by 1.9 percent by 2020. Food prices have risen and then plummeted after the advent of the virus. Out of the total population of the 38 million Afghans almost 4 million population was displaced of which almost 1 million were those displaced due to natural disasters, like floods and droughts. Increased violence has resulted in a dramatic increase in the number of displaced individuals over the last year. In Iran and Pakistan, an extra 2.5 million Afghan refugees have been registered. Violence, drought, and the coronavirus epidemic, according to the World Food Program, might starve up to 14 million Afghans. Aside from the current humanitarian situation, the West, as well as other countries such as Russia and China, is concerned about Afghanistan's drug trafficking dependence. The Taliban have requested international assistance in helping poor people overcome their opium addiction.

Afghanistan has received more than € 4 billion in EU development aid since 2002, making it the world's largest beneficiary. During the 2020 Afghanistan Conference in Geneva, the European Union authorized an additional €1.2 billion in financial help for Afghanistan. However, EU assistance was contingent on a comprehensive Afghan-led peace process at the time. The partnership in development has come to an end. The European Commission has stated that it will deliver more than € 200 million in humanitarian aid to Afghanistan by 2021, more than three times the amount previously provided, in response to the country's escalating humanitarian catastrophe.

The EU has made it plain that any future engagement with the Afghan government must be based on a peaceful and comprehensive accord, as well as respect for all Afghans' fundamental rights, including women's, youth's, and minorities' rights. Its international responsibilities include fighting corruption and preventing terrorist groups from entering Afghanistan. On June 10, 2021, the European Parliament passed a resolution on the situation in Afghanistan, expressing worry about the repercussions of troop withdrawal. He also advocated for the establishment of a long-term EU-Afghanistan partnership.

1.3.2 India-Pakistan Escalation:

1.3.2.1 Relationship between Pakistan and India

In 1947 Pakistan and India both got independence from Britain. After the independence both countries have several other reasons of conflict among them however, the most prominent conflict was on territory which leads to the annexation of Jammu and Kashmir (Qadir, 2002). During partition it was claimed that one will be land for Muslims and the other will be Hindu's state and Kashmir beings a Muslim state must be absorbed in Pakistan while on the other hand, the Indian government stated that Kashmir's Hindu monarch had acceded to India and that a vote was superfluous. The first Indo-Pak conflict, which started in 1948, saw Kashmir partitioned into two parts: "Pakistani-administered Kashmir and Indian-administered Kashmir". However, both states were not pleased on this division as this led to another war among both nations which held in 1965. This war comes to an end when both nations signed a treaty to take care of their bilateral concerns and try to resolve those (Oh et al., 2011). They started a third war in 1971, which ended in Pakistan's breakup, with Bangladesh emerging as a free state that had previously been a part of Pakistan (Hussain & Iqbal, 2018).

Since the 1970s, the two countries have been engaged in an arms race in which they have invested substantially in missile and nuclear technologies. After atomic bombs were detonated in the late 1990s, they became nuclear-capable countries. Even nuclear deterrence was ineffective, and the two nations fought their fourth war, known as the Kargil War, in 1999. However, due to international pressure, the violence remained confined to Kashmir and did not spread to other parts of the country (Rabasa et al., 2009). Recently there occur many dramatic escalations among the said nations during these two decades along with these four major wars. Three significant vicious episodes in which India has blamed Pakistan for helping with aggressors are the "attacks on the Indian parliament in 2001, the Mumbai attack in 2008, and the Uri assault in 2016" (Mathur, 2017). Pakistan has likewise blamed India for supporting and abetting the Pakistani Taliban, who have completed many destructive assaults in the country (Hussain et al., 2021). Pakistan additionally blames India for aiding rebels in the area of Balochistan, which is wealthy in natural resources (Hussain and Lynch, 2019).

When Pakistan and India displayed their nuclear capabilities in 1998, it was thought that this would help to ease the tensions between the two countries to some extent. Aside from that, nuclear deterrence was established in the hopes of ending all sporadic skirmishes and assisting in the maintenance of peace in South Asia. It is self-evident that nuclear powers have the ability to either destroy or maintain peace. When both countries became competing nuclear powers, there was hope that no one would become involved in a conventional war because such a conflict would result in massive destruction. Regardless of these circumstances, both countries become involved in competition, either directly or indirectly, as evidenced by the Kargil battle, the 00-2002 standoff, the Mumbai crisis, and the most recent Pulwama issue, which is the focus of this paper. The most recent India-Pakistan confrontation occurred on 14 February 2019 in Pulwama, where over 40 troops were killed and more than 70 were injured in a suicide attack (Jonana et al., 2019). The terrorist group Jaish-e-Mohammad claimed responsibility for the attack. In response, India's air forces launched an attack in Balakot on February 26, 2019, which was identified as the Jaish-e-training Mohammad's complex. This was the first air strike following the war of 1971, in response to which Pakistan launched an air strike of its own, resulting in an air combat on both sides and the downing of an Indian fighter plane. To end the crisis, the administration released the pilot, which calmed the situation and prevented both countries from succumbing to mass weapon destruction.

1.3.2.2 Surgical Strikes and the Palwama Attack

The Palwama attacks happened in the Indian-led Kashmir as a result India retaliate and the result was the surgical strikes in Pakistan which Pakistan called a war crime, were two recent events that strained already strained relations (Al Jazeera, 2019). A militant group attacked the Indian army on 14th February 2019 at the area of Palwama, as a result 40 Indian soldiers were killed. India blamed Pakistan for this tragedy. In response Pakistan offered a cooperative investigation of the incidents to find out the real culprit. The offer was rejected by India, and they prepared for the surgical strikes in Pakistan for removing the militant camps (BBC, 2019). India launched airstrikes in Pakistan on 26th of February 2019 due to which large number of militants were killed (The Hindu, 2019). Whereas Pakistan confirms such airstrikes from India side, but they also claimed that there observed no damage as a result of this strike. However, such strikes give rise to the boarder violence among both nations (BBC, 2019). On

27th February 2019, also sent the airstrike in Kashmir and also Pakistan destroyed the mainstream India and caught its Wing Commander Abhinandan Varthaman. Pakistan at first disproved India's case, however later conceded that one of its pilots had disappeared and had been captured by Pakistan (The Hindu, 2019). The standard and online media in the two nations shrouded the occasions exhaustively, with a solid feeling of nationalism (Al Jazeera, 2019). Sunrise, a significant Pakistani paper, hammered the media war, foreseeing that an atomic clash between atomic furnished nations would bring about all out demolition (Dawn, 2019). By exploring the Palwama occurrence in two of Pakistan's principal papers, Tribune and Dawn, we assess the degree and nature of data warfare at national level.

1.4 Problem Statement

It has been evident that credibility is one of the most important factors of the news media. People also prefer those mediums of information only by which they can get reliable information. In the way, extensive literature reveals that only a credible source of information gain people's attention. Studies carried out by Lankes (2007) maintained that with the emergence of technological boom people's perceptions towards credibility changes and internet enables people to get information from different sources by which they can check the credibility of information and source. The time period of 1998-2008 has been regarded as the era of decline of credibility of every news media (Pew Research Center, 2008). Also, studies carried out by Arabi (2012) found that whenever there occurs decline in the credibility of news media people often try to find out the source which will be more credible. Due to this reason, it has been found that numerous formal institutions in the world have been suffered from the severe damages likewise the security forces of Pakistan in its history claimed a serious challenge on its writ which later as defined in the context of miscommunication. In the regard, credibility serves as a catalyst for enhancing the smooth working of the institutions and pave the way for their growth and development.

Therefore, for determining the credibility of key events in mainstream media study will contrast the framing of two main events of both national and international importance i.e., Palwama attack leading to 27 February Pak-India escalation and US withdrawal from Afghanistan. For the purpose, study is investigating the two main English newspapers of the country i.e., the Tribune and Dawn on those incidents in the print media of Pakistan for analyzing the framing context of these news agencies. In this way, study is motivated to analyze the framing of the importance of national and international incidents in the print media of Pakistan.

1.5 Research Questions

Research questions of the underlying study are as follow:

- How the Dawn and Tribune have framed the Palwama attack leading to 27 February Pak-India escalation in their newspapers?
- How the Dawn and Tribune have framed the US withdrawal from Afghanistan in their newspapers?

1.6 Aim & Objectives

Based on the following research questions, *aim and objectives* of the underpinned study are;

The study *aims* to evaluate and analyze the framing of print media of Pakistan by taking the consideration from 27th February Pak-India escalation and US withdrawal from Afghanistan based on which the research objectives are:

The study has *objectives* to;

- Review the importance of issue in the print media.
- Understand the framing analysis of print media of Pakistan with special emphasis to Dawn and Tribune media groups.
- Examine how the incidents of national and international relevance are framed in Pakistan's print media.
- Evaluate and analyze the framing of Palwama attack leading to Pak-India Escalation in the Dawn and Tribune newspapers.
- Evaluate and analyze the framing of US withdrawal from Afghanistan in the Dawn and Tribune newspapers.
- Analyze the topics, sources and frames based on which the print media (the Dawn and Tribune) has reported the incidents (Palwama and US withdrawal).
- Analyze the credibility of Pakistan's print media in framing the national and international importance events.

1.7 Hypothesis of the Study

The *hypotheses* of the study are.

- Print media of Pakistan is a credible source for highlighting both national and international incidents.

- It is more likely that different print media organizations have the different framing criterion for framing the national and international incidents.

1.8 Significance of the Study

Studies carried out by Mushtaq (2015) found that in a developing country like Pakistan private news media is growing largely which was further supported by Haque (2013) in his study where he maintained that as traditional media loses its insights private media take over its place. The underlying reason behind this is the biasness of traditional media towards specific political groups due to which these loses their credibility. Present research is based on the credibility theory and framing theory where the researcher tries to investigate the credibility of two important sources of information transfer i.e., the DAWN and Express TRIBUNE. The study will analyze the most credible source of information and will try to explore the reasons due to which the source will be considered reliable. Also, it tends to analyze that which media source is preferred by the public and why. Additionally, the study will try to figure out the credibility framing of national and international events in the national print media agencies. Therefore, study have the keen importance for its readers, students, and researchers.

1.9 Outline of the Study

This thesis is organised into five chapters that are an introduction, literature review, methodology, results and discussions and the conclusion and recommendations. All of these five chapters have their significance and motivated to explain the theme of underpinned research in different ways.

In the first chapter of the research, the researcher has given the overall introduction of the study in which he has discussed the background of the whole concept along with sharing its significance. Moreover, to find out the core elements of the research, he has made some research questions that helped in driving the whole research as per the proposed aims and objectives of the research. Moreover, the chapter has also given the novelty of this research and has mentioned the hypothesis that has directed the researchers in accomplishing the whole context of the research. In the second chapter, the researcher has consulted the extensive literature that are extracted from relevant sources to conceptualize the whole concept of the research. The secondary data tends to provide support and let the researcher get acknowledged with the existing knowledge so that he can further drive the research in another or similar context.In the third chapter of the research, the researcher tends to mention the complete methodology of the research. The third chapter, methodology helps in designing the research accordingly. It tends to provide a structure as per which, the researcher can direct his research and have coherence in it. In this research, the researcher has mentioned that what approaches he has used to explore the site and the context of the research. Moreover, he mentions that which philosophies support his research topic and which methods of the data collection has he used. Furthermore, he has also given the limitation of the research along with discussing the ethical considerations that he has made while framing the research.In the fourth chapter, the researcher has given the analysis of his primary as well as secondary data that he has collected with regards to the topic. For this, he has given qualitative data along with some statistical evidence that he has gathered *through primary or secondary research analysis.In the last chapter of the research, the researcher has given the concluding remarks on the overall findings of the research. He has summarized the whole research in that chapter and based on the conclusions that are derived from the findings of the research, he has proposed some recommendations as well as policies so that improvements can be made to resolve the issue that has been addressed in the underpinned study.*

CHAPTER TWO

LITERATURE REVIEW

2.1 Overview

The importance of literature reviews compelled researcher to do in-depth analysis of the issue under consideration for which researcher go through extensive prior work. For the relevant literature review various sources were used i.e., journals, articles and websites of the relevant newspapers. This chapter has been segregates into parts where section 1 will present the general overview for understanding the motive of the study. Section 2 will present the conflict situation and role of media. Section 3 of the study will present the importance of framing in mass media. Section 4 will shed a light on the importance of credibility and the role of print media in the context of said issue.

2.2 Introduction

This study is primarily concerned to analyze the situation of conflict and the role of print media where the researcher has selected an important source of mainstream media i.e., Newspaper. To determine the framing of national and international incidents in mainstream media and for assessing the importance print media researcher will discuss two main incidents of the national and international importance for the country i.e., US withdrawal from Afghanistan and the Pak-India escalation leading to Pulwama attack. By discussing these incidents, the study will analyze the role and credibility of newspapers in the framing of such incidents.

According to Tewksbury and Schenfele (2008), different researchers believe that framing effects are always the outcome of general public exposure to mass media because it has the ability to modify our opinions about particular subjects and occurrences. According to several studies, individuals are heavily reliant on the media for information, and it plays a significant influence in shaping their perspectives of the conflicts about which they obtain information through the media. Different contending parties employ various forms of media for various goals. Peleg (2006) claims that the media plays a significant role in resolving various conflicts. Furthermore, some experts regard the media as a two-edged blade that has the ability to both transmit tension around the world and deescalate certain crises (Patel, 2004). In the light of media, this form of conflict in the media can be easily defined through framing. Salman Yousaf (2015) did a thorough investigation into public perceptions of Pakistan in the United States and China's news media. The study's major goal was to look into how the Chinese Xinhua and the American Associated Press framed Operation Zarb-e-Azb. The data for this study was collected from May 15 to July 15. It was discovered that the American Associated Press and Chinese Xinhau frame Zarb-e-Azb differently in respective news organizations. The study went on to say that these disparities may be found in how countries deal with terrorism, international relations, and economic viewpoints, and that this framing process is influenced by the countries' vested interests in international politics. According to a study, China and the United States used five different news frames when framing Pakistani news in their news agencies. A terrorism threat frame, a domestic politics frame, an economics consequence frame, an international relations frame, and a social frame are among these frameworks.

Terrorism threat frames, according to Papacharissi & de Fatima Oliveira (2008), have components that give them news value and keep them in the mainstream media. Similarly, the economic ramifications influence how news is presented in the media. According to Neuman, Just, and Crigler (1992), the economic consequence frame has its own position in the media because it is ordinary news. When the host country is confronted with public relations issues that are fundamentally political in nature, the domestic frame is the prevailing frame (Yao, 2010). Social context. This frame includes stories on Pakistan's social life, culture, art, and people during the recent wave of terrorism and religious extremism.

The social frame is a key frame in news coverage of issues that have a significant impact on ordinary people's lives (Sern & Zainuddin, 2012). Frame for international relations. This frame contains stories about Pakistan's diplomatic relations with other countries. In the media research of global challenges such as global warming, international relations have been a dominant framing (Brossard, Shanahan, & McComas, 2004). Credibility has remained an important aspect of mass communication since it is founded on and influences the perceptions of the general public. A brand, or anything else, will be credible

if it follows three characteristics, according to Hoffler and
Keller (2002): knowledge, likeability, and trustworthiness.
There is a lot of study on the credibility of non-media
items (Edrem, 2004), but only a little empirical research on
the credibility of news media (Oyedeji, 2009). In the news
media, credibility is described as a quality of a message
source that can be classified into two categories: higher
credible sources and lower credible sources (Oyedeji,
2010). Bucy (2003) asserted that in mass communication,
credibility can be abstracted as the general public's
impression of a particular source of news. Gaziano and
McGrath (1986) developed a scale for measuring media
credibility, which has been regarded as the first approach
to the measurement of media credibility. Meyer (1988)
created a measure of credibility that included two factors:
affiliation and the amount of belief. Furthermore, Oyedeji
(2006) expanded Meyer's concept of the credibility scale
by defining it on two essential scales: media source
accuracy and public trust in sources.

With these observations in mind, the researcher will
examine the credibility of general news outlets in the
country in the context of two major historical events that
will be discussed in the following sections.

2.3 Role of Mass Media

According to Hooghiemstra (2000), "media is the most
important form of communication". Similarly, according to
a study by Bernstein (1984), mass media is basically a
platform where institutions form an image, with all
strategies being the responsibility of the agency's public
relations function. Examples include phrases used in
advertising, literature, or advertisements. The stories found

led the researcher to Collier (1967), who argued that the use of image display at multiple points and scenarios would be long-term and constructive. According to Lippmann (1922), images are experienced in the public consciousness as a reaction to images. He says that people will first notice and notice, rather than first seeing and then describing. Due to its complexity, Lippmann coined the term "pseudo environment" to describe how people relax the existing environment into a more humid version. A three-way relationship is formed between "display", "perception of human vision" and "human response to perception associated with vision" as the human mind eventually creates a reliable representation of the external world. As a result, he argued that people's reactions to current situations are influenced by their past experiences or the way the image is presented. The socio-psychological dimensions of the nation's image have been studied in several studies. According to the literature, fictional images are described as "Ontism and the formation of emotions and behavioral assessments before having an inner vision of the self and the environment" (Boulding, 1956). This is an ordered representation of an object in the mental structure of a person. The myth of an image is an observable characteristic of the element with which it is associated (Merritt and Deutsch, 1965).

The product can be a company or a country (Boulding, 1956). The national image, according to Konjic, is a mental representation of a country and its people that a person carries in their mind and finds fascinating (1997). have a duty to create 'Suspicious weather' as a result of Studies by Lippmann (1922) found that the most lasting consequences are the stereotypes in a person's mind, using what he / she can frame the world before he / she sees it. Perlman and Cosby (1981) in their study define stereotypes as a set of characteristics associated with a particular social group, according to which they see the world around them. They are our public declarations to the world about our beliefs, attitudes, and civil liberties (Lippmann, 1922). A party worldview that reveals the state of mind, the system of social perceptions of the faith movement, and the ties between nations, tribes and groups. This can be linked to the establishment of the group itself as the center of everything: everything is judged and judged. In reference to him (LeVineand Campbell, 1972). Most image philosophers are interested in the intellectual impact of group membership. They discovered that the notion of collective belonging to a country influences important reactions to the images that we see in the world. According to Alexander and Leon (2005), the image or perception of one country in relation to another is based on three auxiliary components of daytime conditions: "objective similarity, comparative strength, and comparative social status or complexity".

The assessments that lead to these structural linkages will determine the kind of images known as accessory, rivalry, savage, imperialist, and reliant pictures, and thus can change companionable global customs. Another group of researchers looked for elite (Wang, 2000) and popular (Huck, 1984) perspectives on a country. In the mid-1990s, Wang looked at the shared perceptions of Chinese and American elites. He thought that nation image refers to each country's impression of its worldwide political rival's character, which he described as prejudiced, established, and unambiguous. These are linked to stereotypes about people, countries, and nations that are influenced by historical events and mental self-image. Similarly, some academics are fascinated by the process of image formation. For instance, White (1999) developed two models that were concerned with establishing image formation, which tends to describe Australians' perceptions of China. One of these models was central, and it was expected to provide multidimensional images, with a multifarious culture that was profound in both inner and exterior experiences. The second model of the study, on the other hand, was concerned with providing another interdisciplinary structure that tends to invigorate the intercultural perceptive with the use of images that tend to connect distinct learning portions within a human mind. Furthermore, most academics agree that elites' perspectives influence their leadership in interactions with other countries (Hoffmann, 1968), and hence influence bilateral relations between states (Alexander et al., 2005).

2.4 Media and Terrorism

The development of terrorist actions in recent years, which also gave rise to journalism, has made it difficult for journalists to recall numerous norms of ethics. However, a number of studies are interested in how the general public views terrorist threats and how they will respond to existing information about these threats. A variety of materials about how the media portray terrorist events in their own perspective and manner may be found on various websites. As the media is always responsible for their intelligence actions as well as the information they cover and deliver to the public, some experts argue that the media should establish the standard for reporting terrorist attacks. Terrorist organisations use the media to disseminate their ideology, according to Free and Rohner (2007), and the media uses information about terrorists in the same way that the media's audience grows in the aftermath of a terrorist incident. Terrorist acts in poor nations are "bloodier" than in the United States or Europe because it is a game of common interest or common interest where the media and terrorists win. According to Burakowski, the terrorists want the media to publicize their story since it has helped them gain popularity. Send a message to the government, requesting that they pay attention to your programme (2013). The media makes these terrorists prominent, but "there is no evidence that media coverage of terrorists enhances popular sympathy," as Bruce Hoffman (2006) points out. Terrorists and media experts, as well as terrorist groups whose names emerge on the front pages of television shows, talk shows, or newspapers in their early stages, get public exposure and enlighten the public and government about their goals and ideologies. This is a fantastic thing to do (Dowling, 1986). According to studies, the media has a long history of irresponsible reporting that has resulted in a number of problems. These are not to be disregarded examples.

This phenomenon, according to Schmidt and De Graaf (1982), explains the alarming media attention. Four terrorists hijacked a British Airways airliner on November 2, 1974, in exchange for the release of 13 terrorists imprisoned in Egypt. Egyptian officials agreed and pledged to free 13 terrorists; however, no terrorists have been released, according to the media. The crooks had been warned. One of the captives was slain in the process. Many studies (Magwen, 2008) as well as Norris et al. Those involved in terrorist activities are said to have been injured (2002). Terrorist attacks are linked to an increased risk of post-traumatic stress disorder and other illnesses. Four terrorists hijacked a British Airways airliner on November 2, 1974 and liberated 13 terrorists held in Egypt. The Egyptian authorities agreed and pledged to free 13 terrorists, according to the media. The terrorists, on the other hand, are not released, the kidnapper is alerted, and the hostages are slain. Observers affected by terrorist operations, according to several studies (Maguen, 2008) and Norris et al. (2002). Terrorist attacks have been related to an elevated incidence of PTSD and other disturbing symptoms. Hundreds of millions of Americans regularly watch television coverage of 9/11 and the Iraq war. The coverage of 9/11 and the Iraq war in the media has also exacerbated PTSD (payment). The media's portrayal of heinous acts of violence instils anxiety and worry in people who aren't directly injured or in danger. While this is true, it is vital to remember that the media's primary objective is to inform the public. Despite the fact that the majority of studies on terrorist incident coverage are negative, experts believe there are particular cases and features where media coverage might be beneficial. Two factors will be addressed in this research. There are always ups and downs in the media world. The media, on the other hand, can be assumed to have a substantial impact on people's lives because it contributes to the formation of people's thoughts and attitudes. The press must be extremely cautious about what it publishes and how it publishes it.

2.5 Landscape of Pakistani Media

The Pakistani media has gained worldwide recognition for her excellent performance and outspoken independence. It is also worth noting that elves have always been censored by the domestic media, given the role of the military and media organizations working for the state. In addition, ISI, Pakistan's most dangerous and globally recognized organization, has significant control over the country's print media. Control and manage your print media. Urdu is particularly popular as it is spoken by the vast majority of Pakistanis (INFOASAID, 2012). Journalists were banned from examining defamed military activities in Balochistan, the Federal Tribal Areas (FATA), and Khaybar Pakhtunkhwa by Pakistan's "deep state." Simultaneously, the media play a vital role in covering uncontrolled manipulation, if any, at all times, as well as in assisting in the understanding and disclosure of activists' commitments and commitments in a variety of activities, both locally and worldwide. It can be dangerous if you don't use good self-censorship and follow Deep State principles. Because Pakistan's intelligence services are accustomed to issuing cautionary statements. including the use of lethal force to quiet military and intelligence foes Journalists are threatened by both state and non-state entities (Hussain and Jahanzeb, 2014).

The Government of Pakistan maintains considerable control over the media by spending heavily on publicity and public awareness. The government also influences daily life by limiting the supply of paper by manipulating prices and a selective cap. For example, after China which is the largest urdu newspaper and The News newspaper which is an English newspaper Publish an article criticizing the management. The government has withdrawn large public subsidies for advertising. The government sent Jung's company tax returns for a total of $ 13 million, pressured a group of government inspectors, and denied the group access to acceptable newspapers to avoid publishing negative articles about the government. etc.,

2002). The Pakistani military claimed responsibility for the attacks during the early years of the drone programme, which is crucial for our inquiry. Hayatullah Khan, a freelance photojournalist from Miram Shah in North Waziristan, revealed the falsehood by uploading footage of the Hellfire missiles used in the December 1, 2005 death of Al Qaeda members in Miram Shah. As a result, Hayatullah Khan and his brother were kidnapped. Khan, who formerly worked for the Ausaf daily as an Urdu-language correspondent, said he received threats from Pakistan's military and security forces, as well as the Taliban and residents. Hayatullah Khan was slain, but his brother lived to tell the story to future journalists who were interested in learning more about military drones (Shah et al., 2002). Under the guise of 'undesirable behavior,' international journalists who criticize the military, other government agencies, and even the civilian administration are barred from entering Pakistan, while Pakistani journalists are forbidden from calling any of these important actors, threatening death or injury (Singh, 2012).

Besides the thematic exclusion zones, Pakistan has geographical exclusion zones. With the exception of a few journalists with tribal ties to one of the various tribal agencies, Pakistani journalists are generally barred from entering FATA. Another place where journalists are barred from entering is Baluchistan, Pakistan's largest but least densely populated province. Baluchistan has been divided into ruthless rebel movements filled with racial unrest and allegations of human rights violations (SPDC, 2012). It is also the site of the so called "Quetta Shura", which provides a safe haven for senior Taliban commanders as well as government support. Although many other forms of media are available in Pakistan, television is the most widespread.

Pakistan Television Company (PTV) is the only television broadcaster in the country.

Satellite, cable, or Internet TV must be used by all private broadcasters. According to Gallup Pakistan, more than 48 million of Pakistan's 86 million television viewers could only watch free PTV news as a result of this (UNOCHA, 2014). Private radio stations are prohibited from airing national news, with a few exceptions. The government's Pakistani Broadcasting Corporation has a near-monopoly on rural radio listeners, with the exception of rebels who use radio stations to frighten and control the local populace. Radio is especially important in rural regions where electricity and television are rare; nonetheless, when television is available, Pakistanis prefer it to radio. Even though the Internet is becoming a more valuable resource in Pakistan, just 16% of the population has access to it (UNESCO, 2014). Despite Pakistan's low internet penetration, the government has restricted access to certain online resources, including YouTube, due to concerns over overt content. Websites linked to the treatment of minorities in Baluchistan and Pakistan have previously been blocked by the government. As other forms of media have become more readily available, newspapers and print media have lost their appeal. In the late 2000s, the number of print periodicals exploded, reaching 1,820 in 2007. However, it has been progressively reducing since then, falling to 646 in 2012. Fazmaleh Shah (Shah Fazmaleh, 2002). Newspapers, on the other hand, performed better with varying circulations, but have consistently increased since 2001. Cindy suffered the biggest loss in newspaper circulation, the fewest were printed, and only 75 publications. Surprisingly, Baluchistan has a large number of newspapers, about 340 in 2012, which is twice as many as Punjab, i.e., owns 152 newspapers.

Pakistani publications and magazines include 469 newspapers in Urdu and 681 newspapers in English. Nevertheless, Urdu newspapers are still popular. In 2008, 3 out of 4 newspapers were bought in Urdu (4.6 million per day). The two most commonly used typing languages are Sindhi and English. Given that all newspapers are regularly read by many, the actual number of media subscribers is clearly higher than stated. According to INFOASAID (2012), the most read newspaper in Pakistan is Daily Jang, a conservative Urdu daily with an estimated readership of 850,000 in 2012. In second place is the conservative Urdu newspaper Nawa-i-Waqt, which has a circulation of about 500,000. Dawn is the oldest and most widespread English-language newspaper. With 138,000 copies sold, mostly in the city. Dawn's progressive content is well known. Dawn's website receives 10 million views per month, according to INFOASAID (2012). Jang Media Group owns The News, the second most popular English newspaper. These journals are also available online for free, as well as print distribution. Most assessments of Pakistan's media environment ignore how much Pakistanis trust these many news sources for local, national, regional and global events, let alone how much they trust them. Adil et al. (2015) examined the customs of the Pakistani media as well as the awareness and opinion of US drone operations in the country.

Fair et al. (2015) performed a representative survey with 7,648 respondents in four Pakistani provinces: Punjab, Sindh, Baluchistan, and Khyber Pakhtunkhwa in the autumn of 2013. We looked at the three primary media sources that Pakistanis utilize to receive information about happenings in local communities, as well as events in Pakistan and abroad, using this information. This is the latest news source to provide information about Pakistan's drone program. We also looked at three main sources of news that respondents used to keep abreast of recent developments. In this survey, 4,939 (65%) people had heard of the U.S. drone program and 2,709 (35%) had not. The majority of those who heard of the initiative said they supported it "not at all" or "somewhat", while 15% said they supported it "a lot" or "a little". Ordinary Pakistanis seldom, if ever, read newspapers; instead, the country's media elite devours them and the political signals they convey. The information elites then spread it via formal and informal channels. Some members of the media elite who write for newsrooms also contribute to Pakistan's public and commercial television programs as news anchors or regular guests on news programs. As a result, editorials in newspapers inform and reflect the different viewpoints and news frameworks provided by many news outlets in Pakistan, creating a flow of information that ultimately reaches the average Pakistani. Newspaper editors working in both print and broadcast media can be found in many places. Ejaz Haider, well-known English newspaper commentator who directs the Urdu news program 'Belaag' on Capital TV; 26 Moeed Pirzada, journalist of various backgrounds in English publications. There are just as many different backgrounds in Pakistan. Urdu news channel for private channels and PTV; Najam Sethi, a well-known English newspaper commentator who directs the "Aapis ki baat" news program on Geo News; Najam Sethi, famous commentator in English newspapers, who runs a news program called "Aapis ki baat" `on Geo. Ahmed Qureshi is a presenter of Urdu language television channel Express

News and also a columnist for Urdu language newspaper Jang and English the News.

2.6 Background Knowledge on the Selected Issues

In this study as the two prominent incidents were selected i.e., US withdrawal from Afghanistan and Pak-India escalation leading to Palwama Attack. Therefore, following section will present the literature on these two events.

2.6.1 Background of US Withdrawal from Afghanistan

The United States commemorates 20 years since the terrorist attacks of 11 September 2021, which ended two decades of military involvement in Afghanistan. Despite the fact that US and Allied forces have left Afghanistan, there are still fears about the country's long-term destiny. The Taliban's quick gains in territory and control of vital supply routes, border crossings, and provincial capitals has stoked fears that the group could capture control of the country and extend the civil war.

2.6.1.1 Afghanistan and the observed interventions

United States and its allies are conducting various militant operations in Afghanistan since October 2001 which led to the interventions in Afghanistan. At that time, it was observed that various military actions were initially carried out by the US-led coalition which was termed as the self-defense under UN charter. At the same time on 12th September 2001 NATO uses its article V which has the collective defense clause. In 2001 there observed the deployment of ISAF which contains 5000 troops for the purpose of providing aid to the country's security and reconstruction. Despite the UN mandate, the ISAF continues to operate as a coalition of the willing. In the United States, counter-terrorism activities were kept separate from Operation Enduring Freedom.

NATO took responsibility of ISAF in August 2003.[1] ISAF operations spanned the country throughout the next decade, strengthened by a revived and extended UN mandate, and progressed from security and stability to combat and counterinsurgency operations, and finally to transition.

1 Timeline of major force decisions

- October 2001 – Operation Enduring Freedom begins.
- December 2001: UN authorises the International Security Assistance Force (ISAF).
- August 2003 – NATO assumes ISAF command.
- June 2006 – ISAF mandate expanded.
- 2009 –counterinsurgency operations begin.
- 2011-2014 – Three-year transition to Afghan-led security operations.
- October 2014- end of UK combat operations.
- December 2014 – end of combat operations, withdrawal of ISAF.
- 1 January 2015 – Afghan forces assume security responsibility. NATO establishes Resolute Support Mission.
- February 2020 – peace agreement reached between the US and the Taliban
- April 2021, US and NATO announce revised withdrawal plan.
- 1 May 2021- Coalition forces begin withdrawing, to be complete by 11 September 2021.

Figure 1 Timeline of major force decisions

ISAF has around 132,000 troops at its peak in 2011, along with the militants from the all partner countries of NATO.[2] The number of troops on the ground fluctuated depending on the security situation. The coalition's combat activities, including the US operation Enduring Freedom, came to a conclusion on December 31, 2014. NATO moved to a new non-combat mission called deployable support when the Afghan National Security Forces seized authority of security in Afghanistan on January 1, 2015. The primary purpose of Resolute Support was to support the "Afghan National Security Forces; Freedom Sentinel replaced Operation Freedom Sentinel, which contributed to Resolute Support, while retaining US counterterrorism operations in Afghanistan (roughly 2,000 aircrew personnel)".

2.6.2 *Peace Deal and Withdrawal Commitments*

President Donald Trump promised to rid the United States of "endless war" in February 2019, but an administration that has begun efforts to reach a peace deal with the Taliban will end in September 2019. However, the organization continued negotiations in February 2020 and announced that an agreement had been reached. Under the agreement, the United States promised to reduce its military presence in the country from 13,000 to 8,600 troops, withdraw its troops from five military zones in 135 days (with the same decline in US leadership) and withdraw all forces by May 1, 2021. In the peace talks, the Taliban promised not to be part of the Taliban or any other al-Qaeda group that the Afghan state would not use to fight those trying to harm the United States. He will also refrain from attending or receiving funding for such events. He went on to say that inter-Afghan peace talks would begin in March 2020. "The agreement between the United States and the Taliban provides a framework for intra-Afghan dialogue with a view to reaching a political solution and a lasting and comprehensive ceasefire," the joint statement said. The Islamic Republic of Afghanistan underlined its willingness to participate in the talks and work with the Taliban to reach a ceasefire accord. The number of US troops stationed in Afghanistan has reduced to around 2,500 by the conclusion of Trump's term in January 2021. An agreement was achieved in December 2020 that could lead to further significant negotiations. However, there will be no progress unless and until President Trump resigns. According to the Pentagon, "any additional payment will be conditional. All parties have prepared to advance the peace process".[3]

2.6.2.1 Biden administration and the US-Afghan Relations

During his presidency, Joe Biden promised that the "Afghan conflict will be brought to a reasonable conclusion". In January 2021, under President Biden, it was announced that "an interagency review of US-Afghanistan policy and terms of the Taliban agreement will be conducted." At the same time, America's goal will remain the same: maintaining peace in Afghanistan. However, given the security situation in Afghanistan, no proper decision was taken regarding the complete withdrawal of US forces from Afghanistan, because the agreements between the two countries did not produce positive results. President Biden presented the future policy of the United States in Afghanistan on April 14, 2021, in which President Biden stated that:

"It is time for US troops to return home and that the United States will fulfill its obligations under the February 2020 agreement," he said. that the threat of terrorists now exists in many parts of the world, and it makes no sense to focus the response on one country alone but instead of ending on that date, the withdrawal procedure would start on May 1, 2021".

He further stated that:

"When I took office I inherited a diplomatic agreement that all American soldiers would be out of Afghanistan on May 1, 2021, just three months after my inauguration, duly negotiated between the United States Government and the Taliban that commitment is something we have inherited".

"It's probably not what I personally would have negotiated until, but it was an agreement from the US government, and it counts for something. As a result, in accordance with this agreement and our national interests, the United States will begin a complete withdrawal on May 1 this year. We do not want to move east." We will do so responsibly, systematically, and securely. And we will do so in close cooperation with our allies and partners in Afghanistan, who now have more troops on the ground than we do. They are completely evacuated".

President Biden said, however, that "the United States would restructure its counterterrorism presence in the region to "prevent the recurrence of terrorists and to monitor and disrupt terrorist networks and operations that have long since overtaken Afghanistan after 9/11".

He further stated that:

"The Taliban will be held accountable for their vote not to allow terrorists to threaten the United States. or its allies from Afghanistan. Beyond the withdrawal, the United States will continue to provide diplomatic, humanitarian and development assistance to the Afghan government, as well as assistance to the Afghan National Defense and Security Forces"

"The war in Afghanistan was never conceived as a multigenerational effort. We were attacked. We enter the battle with specific objectives. These goals have been achieved. Bin Laden dies and al-Qaeda in Iraq and Afghanistan deteriorated and it's time to end the endless battle".

Secretary of State Anthony Blinken repeated the same sentiment the next day at a joint press conference with the Secretary General of NATO and the Secretary of Defense of the United States.

2.6.2.2 The progression of withdrawal Process

The US Central Command has been updating the public on the withdrawal's progress on a regular basis. In its most current report, issued on August 10, 2021, it stated that "the US withdrawal of forces was more than 95% complete and that seven installations had been handed over to the Afghan Ministry of Defense".[4]

This includes the Bagram airbase, which was abandoned on July 2, 2021, by US and NATO troops. The facility was critical to the US campaign in Afghanistan, and the statement ignited hope that the pullout could be finished in a matter of days.

On July 8, 2021, President Biden stated at the White House that "our military engagement in Afghanistan would conclude on August 31".[5]

The Taliban warned that after the May 1 deadline passed, they would no longer be bound by an agreement not to attack international troops. However, there have been no documented cases of Taliban militants attacking coalition soldiers. Any attack on retreating soldiers will be handled with "all the instruments at our disposal," according to US and NATO officials.[6]

2.6.2.3 Protection of US Diplomats

After withdrawal it was decided to leave only 650 US soldiers in Afghanistan for the protection of important units the most important of which was the US embassy which was based in Kabul. At the time Turkey was also in discussions with US and Afghan Government where both were debating to safeguard the Kabul International Airport. However, both does not reach at a specific arrangement. Since 2015, as part of "NATO's Resolute Support mission",[7] the military forces of Turkey were conducting logistic activities at the airport

However, soon after the debates US decided to remove its most of the diplomatic staff till August 31st due to which no decision was made regarding the presence of the US soldiers. John Kirby, a spokesman for the Pentagon, announced at a press conference on August 12:

"Beyond August 31st, I won't guess on what the footprint will look like, how many troops will be present, or what they will be doing."[8]

The Taliban have emphasized that "after the evacuation deadline, no foreign forces, including military contractors, should remain in Kabul. Any foreign troops left in the country will be at risk as occupiers".[9]

2.6.2.4 Afghan National Security Forces

While direct support for the Afghan National Security Forces (ANSF) will end after September 11, 2021, the US has stated that it would continue to help the ANSF through other means.

Officials from the Pentagon announced at a press conference on May 18, 2021, that "support will gradually transition to one of over the horizon support especially in logistics and financial help".

The US has provided funds through the Afghanistan Security Forces Fund to "support the continued development of the ANDSF as an effective and sustainable force with a focus on the ability to sustain high-tempo combat operations against a resilient insurgency and be a reliable counterterrorism partner with the US.[10] The funding for FY2021 is $3.1 billion.[11] The Afghanistan Security Forces Fund received more than $69 billion from the United States between 2005 and 2018".[12]

Administration officials confirmed to the Senate Armed Services Committee on 12 May 2021 that "the US will continue to fund key capabilities such as the Afghan Air Force and Special Mission Wing; and will continue to pay salaries for Afghan Security Forces and continue the delivery of certain military supplies".[13]

The Afghan National Army Trust Fund is another source of revenue for the ANSF.

It is quite likely that contractors will be used to offer maintenance support, particularly to the Afghan Air Force. General McKenzie, the Commander of US Central Command, proposed in a press conference on July 25, 2021 that, going forward:

"We're continuing to offer maintenance and advising them from the horizon, and we're ready to perform over-the-horizon aircraft maintenance and refurbishment with aircraft that will be flown to a third country, fixed, and returned to service with the Afghan Air Force in Afghanistan."[14]

2.6.2.5 Asset Rearrangement in the Fight against Terrorism

For sustaining peace and elevating the terror activities in the region there was need to negotiate with the forces and preserve the over flight rights with neighboring countries. During his presidency Biden encouraged the neighboring countries of Afghanistan to play their active role in maintaining peace and stability in the region. However, it was observed that no countries have the consent to provide their land to US troops for peace maintenance. While it is assumed that for peace maintenance basing in Uzbekistan, Tajikistan, or Kyrgyzstan will be tactically favorable,[15] under such instance. Russia has a sizable presence in the area. Pakistan has already stated that it will not host US troops.[16] According to a recent report by the US Naval Institute:

"For the past 20 years, supporting operations in the Middle East has been a huge drain on carrier readiness, diverting attention away from operations in the Pacific. An assessment of how and where to deploy the stretched US carrier force is part of the ongoing global force posture review".[17]

2.6.3 Alliance groups in Afghanistan

In Afghanistan, it was observed that US and its allies always have taken the approach of "in together and out together"[18] which was further threatening the situations and the peace process failed.

2.6.3.1 NATO's Resolute Support Mission

When US announced to withdraw its security forces from Afghanistan, NATO and its allies at the same time followed their footprints and committed to withdraw their RSM forces, in line with those of its allies. In the regard a statement was presented by the North Atlantic Council on 14 April 2021, the main points of which were as follow:

- "In 2001, for the first time in NATO history, Allies invoked Article 5 of the Washington Treaty and deployed to Afghanistan with clear objectives: to confront al-Qaeda and those responsible for the September 11 attacks, and to prevent terrorists from using Afghanistan as a safe haven to strike us. We have worked together to achieve these aims throughout the decades, investing blood and treasure and partnering with the Islamic Republic of Afghanistan and its security forces".

- "In light of this, and in recognition that there is no military solution to Afghanistan's issues, the Allies have decided to begin withdrawing Resolute Support Mission forces by May 1 [...]"
- "To serve in Afghanistan, NATO built one of the largest coalitions in history. Our troops entered Afghanistan as a unit, adjusted as a unit, and are now leaving as a unit."[19]

NATO members, including the US, went on to say that "withdrawing our troops does not mean that our engagement with Afghanistan is over. Rather, this is the beginning of a new chapter."[20]

The proposal was "not an easy decision, and it carries dangers," according to NATO Secretary General Jens Stoltenberg. "Be prepared for a long-term, open-ended military engagement with maybe more NATO forces," he suggested as an alternative.[21]

The RSM has 17,148 personnel from 39 countries at its peak in June 2019.[22] When NATO's departure pledge was announced in mid-April 2021, the RSM included 10,000 personnel from 36 NATO members and partner countries.[23]

Over the last six months, coalition forces have been steadily withdrawing from Afghanistan. In addition to the United States and the United Kingdom, the following countries are major donors to NATO's Resolute Support Mission:

- On June 29, 2021, Germany (1,300 troops) withdrew the last of its personnel from Afghanistan.
- Italy's (895 troops) disengagement was concluded on June 30, 2021.
- On June 28, 2021, Georgian troops (860) returned home.
- On June 26, 2021, Romania (619 troops) concluded its withdrawal.

Turkey has not yet withdrawn its approximately 600 people from Afghanistan, despite continued discussions about taking over security responsibility for Kabul International Airport (see above).

2.6.3.1 Future NATO support?

The secretary general of NATO said that there will no future support from NATO on the Afghan National Security Forces during its press conference which held on 14th April 2021. However, the plans discussed at this press conference states that:

"It is about continuing to support the Afghan Security Forces, as well as ensuring that we don't endanger the victories won in the battle against international terrorists. We do not know exactly how we'll accomplish it or what role NATO will play but all of these questions are on the table and being debated among NATO allies as well as with Afghanistan".[24]

NATO leaders promised to "continue to provide training and financial support to the Afghan National Defense and Security Forces, including through the Afghan National Army Trust Fund during a Heads of State and Government summit in June 2021. NATO will keep a Senior Civilian Representative's Office in Kabul to maintain diplomatic engagement and strengthen our collaboration with Afghanistan and will provide cash to ensure Hamid Karzai International Airport's continuing operation". NATO has stated that "it will maintain out-of-country training for Afghan security forces, with a special focus on Afghan Special Operations Forces despite the fact that it was not mentioned in the Summit Communique".[25]

NATO officials are said to have approached Qatar about the possibility of establishing a training base there, however it is unclear which NATO countries may be involved.

2.6.3.2 Funding for the National Army of Afghanistan

Under the review of peace talks it was observed that the funds provided by the NATO, US and its allies were supposed to continue i.e., National Army Trust Fund and National Security Forces Funds were said to deliver for aiding the government. The Trust Fund was established in 2007 to give NATO allies, partner countries, and the international community a way to support the ANSF by donating military equipment and funding training.

The Trust Fund has received nearly $3.4 billion in contributions since its inception, as of May 2021.[26]

In the long run, NATO's Enduring Cooperation strategy has reaffirmed NATO's commitment to improving its political partnership with Afghanistan.

2.6.3.3 What does this mean for the military in the United Kingdom?

The entrance of UK in Afghanistan was observed in 2001 where their total of 150610 troops are stationed from last 20 years.[27] During their stay in the Afghanistan more than 600 of the UK troops received serious injuries and 457 were killed.

2.6.3.4 The Military Retreat from Afghanistan and Its Ramifications for Peace

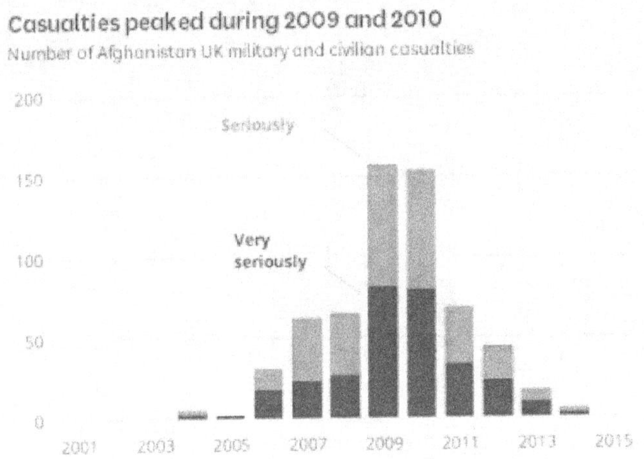

Figure 2 Causalities peaked during 2009-2010

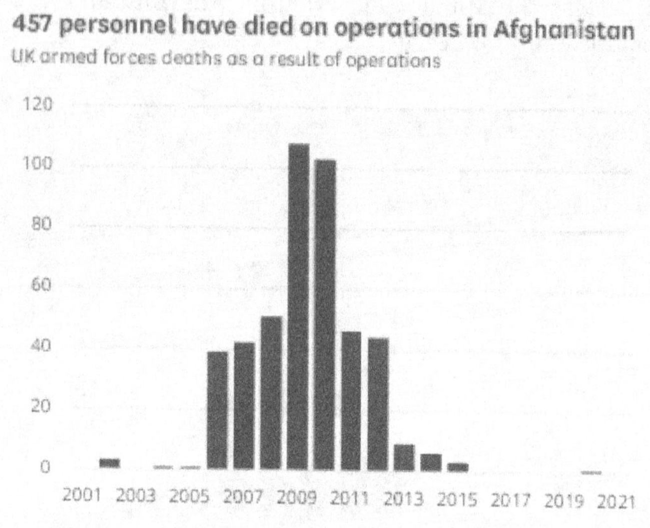

*Figure 3 UK armed forces death as a result of operation
2001-2021*

After observing the serious losses of their people and assets
UK withdrew its troops from Afghanistan in October 2014.
However, by January 2015 it sent its troops again for
assisting the training operation in Afghanistan. By the
beginning of 2021, UK removed all of its troops from
Afghanistan there left only 1100 in Afghanistan.

Following US and NATO troop departure statements,
Defense Secretary Ben Wallace stated that British troops
would leave in accordance with coalition
arrangements.[28] On July 7, 2021, the Prime Minister
testified before the liaison committee, saying:

"If you're asking if I'm happy with the current situation in Afghanistan, the answer is no. I'm a little worried. There are a lot of dangers in this situation. We must hope that the Kabul parties will be able to achieve a deal. We must hope, in some way that a compromise with the Taliban can be reached at some point. We must be completely honest with ourselves about our current situation".

"We must hope that the blood and fortune used by our country over decades to defend the Afghan people was not in vain, and that the memory of their efforts be preserved. That is what our government will endeavor to accomplish, to the best of our ability, alongside our American allies. The situation is difficult."[29]

All British troops assigned to NATO's mission in Afghanistan are now returning home, the Prime Minister declared in a statement on Afghanistan on July 8, 2021.

"I will not reveal our departure schedule for obvious reasons, but I can inform the House that the majority of our people has already left."[30]

2.6.3.5 Role of UK

When the US withdrawal was announced on April 2021, James Heappey who was the minister of armed forces of UK maintained that,

"The UK may have a role in the broader counterterrorism operation being negotiated with the US and NATO allies".[31]

He also stated that:

"Some military equipment would be donated to the Afghan National Security Forces, and that Afghan military personnel may be trained and mentored remotely or on existing military courses in the UK". "Clearly, the military presence in Afghanistan will end, but our capacity to maintain a remote connection to the Afghan military academy, as well as our ability to host Afghan officers and NCOs on military courses

in the UK, will not be affected". "All of this, I believe, will serve to build the links between Afghan and UK armed forces, as well as maintain their capabilities so that they can continue their own operations and achieve a sustainable peace in Afghanistan".[32]

Allies have the right to return to Afghanistan, according to the Minister, "if the security situation deteriorates to the point when our national security is jeopardized".[33]

On July 8, the Prime Minister confirmed that

"UK would continue to financially support the Afghan National Security Forces but gave no further assurances about the UK's future military presence in the region, other than to say that the UK would continue to work with our friends to look at an outside-in approach to counterterrorism".[34]

Several Special Forces personnel have been suggested as being able to stay in Afghanistan in an advice position. The Prime Minister pledged to continue assisting Afghanistan, calling it a *"generational enterprise that now had new tools in our hands".*[35]

He concluded by saying that

"The legacy of the United Kingdom's involvement in Afghanistan is a proud and lasting one. Specifically, millions of children who would not otherwise have been educated. Millions of girls in school who would not otherwise have been in school; the country's terrorist threat being reduced for decades; and, I believe, the possibility of a political, negotiated settlement involving the Taliban, which is the country's only realistic prospect".[36]

2.6.4. Implications for the Peace Process

2.6.4.1 Status of the peace talks

In the view of US and its partners as a result of peace talks now the goals of maintaining peace have been met so there is no need of military presence in Afghanistan. At the time President Biden has stated:

"Continuing to the conditions-based withdrawal policy, which has been the rallying cry for the previous two decades, will result in coalition forces being in Afghanistan indefinitely. Instead, the US and its allies have committed to rebuilding a relationship with Afghanistan based on support for the Afghan government, the peace process, and the Afghan National Security Forces".

On the contrary people were of view that as a result of evacuation of international armed personnel there will be increased worry of peace accord or ceasefire.

2.6.4.2 Status of Peace Talks

By the end of 2020 there were made several arrangements of the peace talks which incorporate some negotiations and the peace talks headed further. By the time there were observed several international initiatives among Taliban and the Afghan government which reap no results and failed. President Ghani outlined a plan for the governance which was named three-point plan. The main motive of this plan was to create a government which by relying on its own framework of the constitution which holds that the government will conclude the presidential elections and reject the demands by US which talks about the constitution of the "interim transitional administration chosen on the concept of equity". Similarly, it also holds that the Taliban will also be scoffed by this strategy.[37]

The Taliban has announced that it will boycott any conference on Afghanistan's future until "all foreign forces have entirely left our nation".[38]

The NATO, US and its allies issued a Communique in early May 2021 which states:

"The immediate resumption, without preconditions, of substantive negotiations on the future of Afghanistan with the goal of developing and negotiating realistic compromise positions on power sharing that can lead to an inclusive and legitimate government and a just and durable settlement."[39]

They also stated that "the troop withdrawal process must not be used by the Taliban as a justification to postpone the peace process," and that "good faith political dialogue must continue in earnest."

According to the Iranian Foreign Ministry, an Afghan government team met with Taliban commanders in Tehran on July 8, 2021, as coalition forces prepare to withdraw, in an attempt to end the ongoing diplomatic deadlock.

Zalmay Khalilzad, who was the US Special Representative for Afghanistan, met to various allies of NATO between 10th and 12th August in 2021. The purpose of this meeting was to support and discuss the peace talks along with conducting further meetings with Taliban and the representatives from the Afghan government. The main motive of such meetings was to reduce the violence in line with promoting the peace by conducting various activities."[40] At the time, Taliban were offered to take an active part in the power by conducting power-sharing arrangements. However, no details were provided publically in the regard. The Taliban were not satisfied by the agreement and they rejected it by stating that "they will only accept a peace settlement if a new Islamic Emirate is established in Afghanistan".

The Taliban's spokesman, Zabiullah Mujahid, stated that

"The Taliban will reject Kabul's offer of power-sharing and a truce. Our goal is to halt foreign meddling and establish an Islamic administration in this country. We are prepared for a truce if they accept this offer. It will not be difficult for us to fight and prolong our jihad [holy war] if Kabul refuses to recognize our demands".[41]

"The international community will not tolerate any administration that wants to take control of Afghanistan by force," the countries and organizations involved in the talks stated.[42]

2.6.4.2 Escalating Violence in the Country

The withdrawal of international military personnel took place not only in the absence of a peace agreement, but also against the backdrop of increasing bloodshed in the country.

The United States estimates that "Taliban attacks on government forces have averaged 80 to 120 per day over the past year.[43] There was a wave of targeted killings by civil society, the media, the courts and the civil administration, especially women". According to a UN study published in April 2021, "the number of people killed and injured in the first three months of this year (1,783 people) was 29% higher than in the same period of 2020". The same report states that "the Taliban and other anti-government forces killed 61%.[44] An attack on a school in Kabul in early May 2021 killed 55 people, mostly girls, and injured hundreds more". Officials in Afghanistan blamed the Taliban for the bombing; however, the Taliban denied any involvement.

Several observers have blamed the Islamic State (IS), which is still active in Afghanistan, including Kabul and Jalalabad in the east. On 14th May 2021 the IS group in Kabul was blamed responsible for the attack on mosque of which it claims the responsibility. As a result of this attack 12 people were killed including those who were praying.

The Islamic State is seen as a strategic rival to the Taliban.

The Taliban is believed to have some 60,000 fighters, making them the strongest since 2001.[45] Over the past year, he has also quickly conquered territory throughout Afghanistan. At the beginning of 2021, more than half of the country was under direct or disputed Taliban control. Most of the areas directly controlled by the Taliban at the time were remote and rural, generally among the poorest parts of the country.[46]

The US National Intelligence Council concluded in April 2021 that the "Taliban is likely to make battlefield victories in the next years and is confident it can achieve military triumph in two to three years". However, according to a revised US intelligence estimate released at the end of June 2021, "the Afghan government could fall apart in six months".[47]

2.6.4.3 Major Taliban Offenses

Taliban has launched the powerful offensive along with the withdrawal of the coalition forces which was predominantly against the government of Afghanistan. Due to offense of Taliban, it was found that many districts of the country were under the control of Taliban especially in the north of country. Keeping in view the scenario the security forces of Afghanistan also left many districts of the country without showing any resistance.[48] At the same time most of the Afghan troops flew to the neighboring countries during the start of July 2021 due to the fear of Taliban control over Afghanistan.[49]

At the time, Hamdullah Mohib, who was the security adviser in Afghan national security, defended Afghan forces, saying the shortage of supplies and ammunition had caused many of the staff to drop out. He denied widespread rumors that Taliban spies had been abandoned.[50]

It took less than a month that the troops of Taliban took control over the country. Also, it captured many of important borders and supply lines which were linking the country to its important neighbors like Pakistan, Iran, etc. Also, they captured many important cities of the country and its important provinces. The main cities captured by Taliban were Kunduz, Kandahar, Heart etc. Similarly, they also attacked other important provincial capitals. Airstrikes on Taliban targets have been carried out by the US military in support of Afghan national forces.

According to an EU official on August 10, 2021, the Taliban currently control roughly 65 percent of the country.[51] The Taliban have "taken more territory in the last two months than at any other time since the US invasion in 2001," according to a Security Council report from August 2021.[52]

US intelligence assessments have reportedly been reduced as a result of the quick loss of terrain and worries about the ANSF's capability. According to US intelligence officials as of August 10, 2021, Kabul could fall to the Taliban in a month to 90 days.[53]

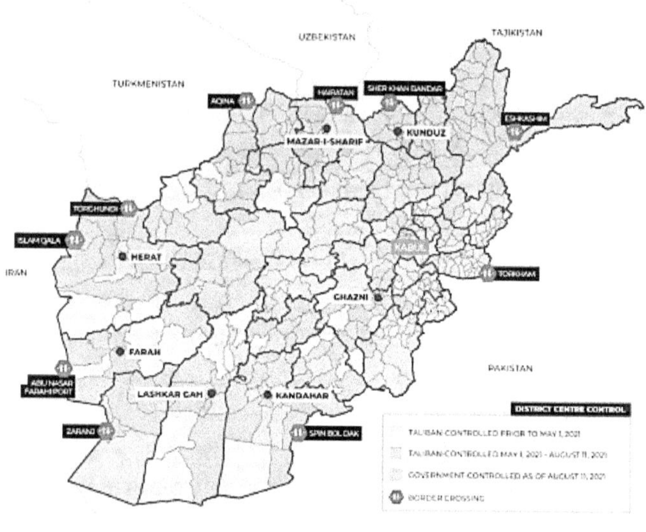

Figure 4 Afghanistan who controls what

Hundreds of Afghan civilians have been killed and many have fled their homes. The UN Refugee Agency warned in July 2021 that Afghanistan was "on the verge" of a humanitarian crisis, estimating that heightened violence had resulted in the displacement of 270,000 Afghans since January 2021.[54]

Michelle Bachelet, the UN High Commissioner for Human Rights, made a statement on August 10, 2021, criticizing the ongoing violence and urging all parties to "stop fighting to avert more tragedy" and come to the bargaining table. She also mentioned reports of Taliban forces committing suspected war crimes and crimes against humanity.[55]

2.6.4.4 Evacuation of US and British Nationals

As the main motive of peace talks was to evacuate the Afghanistan for the purpose the decision was made under which it was stated that the military will leave the land step by step. Such decisions were made after the failure of peace talks held at Doha where the decision was made that the large number of US militant will leave Afghanistan. Along with this it was decided that some additional staff will be deployed from the Afghanistan and Afghan civilian will get a chance to be employed at US and UK, respectively.[56] The US government was of view that the around 3000 military personnel will send to Kabul so that they can help to evacuate the staff employed at US embassy in Afghanistan. The State Department of the United States has stated unequivocally that:

"The embassy is still operating, and we intend to continue working in Afghanistan as diplomats. The US will continue to support consular services, including the processing and operations of the Special Immigrant Visa programme, and will maintain diplomatic relations with the Afghan government and people. In addition, we will maintain our anti-terrorist focus."[57]

"A total of 3,500 military personnel will be deployed to Kuwait and kept on standby in the event that the security situation worsens; 1,000 servicemen will be deployed to Qatar to assist with the migration of former Afghan employees.[58] Any attack on US personnel would be met with a severe and appropriate reaction" according to US military authorities.

UK government also announced that it will withdraw its 600 troops from Afghanistan within a limited time to assist with the evacuation of British people, including embassy workers and contractors.[59]

"The UK Ambassador and his core team of diplomatic workers will relocate within Kabul to a more secure location," according to the government".[60]

2.6.4.5 Warlords in Afghanistan

Afghan militias and former warlords have been rebuilding and remobilizing for months, with many of them organized based on ethnicity. This is especially true in the northern half of the nation, where the Taliban has made the most progress. Fearing the failure of the Afghan National Security Forces (ANSF), the collapse of the Afghan government, and a probable Taliban takeover, several former warlords have sworn to "preserve their areas" if coalition forces depart. "In a scenario where the peace process and the political institutions fail, some factions will rely on these figures for safety," says Ali Adili of the Afghanistan Analysts Network.

Despite President Ghani's objections, the Afghan government has approached Afghan warlords in recent weeks in a bid to strengthen the ANSF and undermine the Taliban's advance. The former Mujahedeen commander and former governor of Herat, Ismail Khan, is said to have led 3,000 soldiers in unsuccessful attempts to secure the city with the Afghan National Security Forces. The Taliban conquered Herat on August 12. President Ghani meets with former warlord and vice president of Afghanistan, General Abdul Rashid Dostum, and local dictator Ata Mohammed Noor, at Mazar-e-Sharif on August 11, 2021, to discuss the city's defense from the Taliban.

The attitude of President Ghani towards the warlords and the other militant groups has appeared as a death of the peace process which questioned the agreements as it focused on uniting the anti-Taliban forces and leaders having common goal of Taliban withdrawal.[61] Former warlords, on the other hand, have a history of shifting allegiances and caring more about protecting their own interests than defending the Afghan government.

According to Ali Adili, "ethnic groups in Afghanistan may want to gain more clout with the Taliban, either during peace talks or if the Taliban take control of the country".[62] The Taliban is said to be reaching out to numerous former Soviet-era mujahedeen factions in order to find common ground and undermine support for the Afghan government.[63] Gulbuddin Hekmatyar, a former mujahedeen leader who is now the head of the Hezb-e-Islami party, is the most renowned. In April 2021, Hekmatyar led a rally in which he declared victory against the Taliban in the Baharak district.[64] Hekmatyar had previously stated that his party was willing to engage in "direct negotiations with the Taliban, as well as collaboration and cooperation," and that "if these two groups join hands, the crisis in Afghanistan would end quickly and no force will be able to stand against it."[65]

As Waleed Mir, writing in The Diplomat in May 2021 observed:

"Kabul will...have to turn a blind eye to their history of human rights abuses, as Waleed Mir wrote in The Diplomat in May 2021. More importantly, Ghani will not forget the rampant side-switching carried out by the same outfits throughout the civil war — all of which allied with the Taliban at least once".

"Whatever happens, the experience of warlords in Afghanistan and elsewhere shows that they are intrinsically dangerous actors. Nonetheless, if the Kabul administration has no other options, they will play a critical role in the future."[66]

2.6.4.6 Prospects for peace?

The start of talks is positive, but questions remain regarding the Afghan government's and Taliban's capacity to reach an agreement on a long-term political settlement and an impending ceasefire. The Taliban is resurgent, and they have no intention of stopping their military onslaught in exchange for a peace settlement. Try to build your own anti-Taliban coalition. Warriors and local militia commanders have been drawn to Afghanistan by the Afghan government.

I'm curious what will happen if the Taliban get control of the country. "In terms of government attitude and strategy, a successful Taliban administration will be comparable to a government that existed before 2001: a conservative religious regime that does not care about development or human rights," says Russia's Nick Reynolds. Indeed, as the Taliban gains momentum, there are more allegations of the Taliban enforcing Sharia law in areas under their control, particularly among women and children.

There are also concerns regarding the Taliban's willingness to cut connections with al-Qaeda and other international terrorist groups like Lashkar-e-Taiba and Jaish Muhammad. Reynolds stated that "NATO's ability to withdraw totally from Afghanistan is impossible and that the future of the United States will either ensure the existence of the Afghan government or back the Taliban terrorist network if they come to power".[67]

Many pundits, on the other hand, feel that the possibilities of Afghanistan devolving into a civil war are significantly higher. They contend that the presence of ISIS in Afghanistan, as well as the interests of surrounding nations in the country, do not make the Taliban's capture inevitable. In contrast to the Taliban's optimism that they can conquer the remaining provincial capitals and Kabul in three months, others, like as former US President Ryan Crocker, fear that the existence of all these warring organizations will lead to a "long and oppressive war".[68]

Afghanistan has long been and remains a battleground for competition from its major neighbors. After the withdrawal of US forces, Afghanistan's neighbors have been able to intensify their power struggles, deepening long-standing national tensions by supporting their proxies. Tajik and Shiite Islam is linked to Hazare Iran. Turkey is a strong supporter of Uzbekistan. While Russia and India have just reconciled with the Taliban, Russia, India and other Central Asian countries can help the Northern Alliance again.[69] India is said to have negotiated with the Taliban in Doha. Pakistan also helps the Taliban find "strategic depth" in the country. China was also open to dealing with the Taliban to prevent border unrest. In response to fears that a possible civil war in Afghanistan could spread to the country's northern neighbors, Russia has pledged to protect its regional partners.[70]

In response to criticism of the present security situation, the US emphasized the Afghan National Security Troops' strong military capabilities, as well as "membranes on the horizon" aid from coalition forces in other regions of the region. During a Pentagon news briefing on August 11, 2021, Press Secretary John Kirby stated:

"No probable scenario, even the loss of Kabul, which everyone appears to be reporting on, has to be inevitable." That does not have to be the case [...]"

"They've... It's basically about having the will and the leadership to leverage those advantages to their own advantage in terms of personnel, operational structure, air forces, and sophisticated weaponry."[71]

President Biden has already stated that the campaign's military objectives in Afghanistan have been met, stating,

"We did not go to Afghanistan to construct a nation and the Afghan people alone have the right and obligation to decide their own destiny and how they wish to rule their country".

President Biden told reporters on August 8, 2021, that he did not regret the decision to withdraw US forces from Afghanistan and that "Afghan leaders must come together [...] they must fight for themselves, fight for their country."[72]

2.6.2 Pak-India Escalation leading to Palwama
2.6.2.1 Introduction

Relations between Pakistan and India have been tumultuous and acrimonious since the partition. The unfortunate fact, according to Mehmood (2002), is that the chances for repairing Pakistan-India ties have always been poor. In 1948, 1965, and 1971, the two nations fought three significant wars. As a result, the two nations have constantly been at odds or in a state of Cold War. Many prominent Indian leaders felt, according to Cameron (2003) that the break was just transitory and that Pakistan, like a prodigal son, would return to India. In 1974, India conducted its first nuclear test, followed by Pakistan, and in 1998, India claimed its first nuclear weapons capability, practically simultaneously with Pakistan. The post-9/11 period is viewed as pivotal in Pakistan-India ties. Due to the quick changes in the global strategic environment as a result of the September 11th events, significant nations have once again been the focus of attention (Ali 2017).

In numerous districts of Mumbai, armed fighters open fire on civilians. On November 26, the world's deadliest terrorist assault occurred. The attack targeted the "Taj Mahal Palace and Tower, Oberoi Trident Hotel, Chhatrapati Shivaji Terminus, Leopold Cafe, Cama Hospital, Nariman House Jewish Community Center, Metro Cinema, St Xavier's College, and an alley near the Times of India's headquarters". Around 160 persons were killed in the attacks. The majority of the killings happened during the Taj siege, which lasted nearly three days and saw shooters imprisoned until one was killed in an Indian security assault.

According to Mahmood (2002), the lone attacker caught alive, Ajmal Kasab, acknowledged to being a Lashkar e Tayiba member (from LeT). The operation was organized and carried out in Pakistan, and all conversations and communications were traced back to that country. India broke relations with Pakistan following the incident. Terrorists dressed as military carried out a catastrophic attack on Pathankot Airport in Punjab, Northwest India, in January 2016. The incident occurs less than a week after Prime Minister Modi made an unscheduled visit to Pakistani Prime Minister Nawaz Sharif in an attempt to restart diplomatic discussions. Terrorists from the JeM assaulted Indian-run military outposts in Uri, Jammu and Kashmir, in September, killing 17 Indian troops. On September 29, India began "surgical strikes" across the Line of Control in Pakistan-administered Jammu and Kashmir in its first direct military reaction to the Uri attack.

2.6.2.2. Palwama Attack

On February 14, in the silence of February, a suicide bomber detonated 300kg of explosives in a car engulfed in a Central Reserve Police Force (CRPF) convoy, killing dozens of Indian officials and wounding hundreds more (Ahmadian and Farahani 2014). The site of the atrocity was Pulwama, about 20 kilometers from Srinagar. India blamed Pakistan for the tragedy and promised revenge and punishment. IJaish e Muhammad has agreed to carry out a terrorist act in exchange for India's liberation from Kashmir. To quell his desire for revenge, the Indian Air Force dropped 1,000 kg of bombs across the LOC, violating the LOC's restrictions. Pakistan then retaliated by kidnapping the Indian pilot and crashing his plane on February 27. Later, to relieve tension and as a goodwill gesture, the pilot was released (Amir Shojaei 2013).

After a violent attack the accusations and convictions began. India has sought to isolate Pakistan internationally through its media (Eissa 2014). The two countries spat at each other with prejudice and threatening words. Arouse the feelings of the opponent Nationalism, religion and culture He used the media as a weapon to showcase and promote a broader ideology and persuade people to accept its views. Religious, political, and social principles are used to describe other countries as the main actors (Tahir 2013).

2.7 Theoretical Framework

Apart from the general security of Pakistan, the topics chosen were a direct concern of the people as they suffered before and after the events started. This study examines how the ISPR presented these episodes, as well as how it influenced the public's perception and opinion of the events in the issue. In developing countries, numerous studies have been conducted on the relationship between the media agenda and the public agenda. When national and international challenges arose, this topic was chosen because agenda setting research with a focus on Pakistan was needed.

2.7.1 Agenda Setting Theory

Agenda theory was founded by McCombs and Shaw in 1972. This theory of communication is concerned with the extraordinary transfer from media representations of the world to representations of our minds. To develop Cohen's point, a key idea with agenda-setting theory is that elements that are prevalent in media images also stand out in images or audience conversations. In the figurative language of concepts, the media agenda determines the public agenda. These programs can hypothetically consist of any component. In fact, most of the research to date has focused on a range of issues of general interest.

The most important theoretical premise of the study was that the amount of attention paid to issues in the media influences the prioritization of these issues by the public (McCombs and Ghanem, 2001). In 1998, McCombs extended the scope of this theory to include the example of 'Framing'. He argued that the media not only taught us what to think, but also how to think about it. The agenda setting process is divided into two phases. The first level refers to the importance of the topic in terms of how information is conveyed in the media. At this level, the media proposes and directs the public's thinking through extensive media coverage. In the second phase of the agenda the media will focus on the nature of the object and its concerns. The media teaches and suggests how people should think about various issues (Yang and Stone, 2003).

2.7.1.1 Media Agenda and Public Agenda

McCombs's agenda-setting concept has been expanded upon by scholars and media experts. In the 1960s, Funkhouser (1973) used agenda theory to examine some of the serious problems Americans face. According to the comparison of public news and public opinion, there is a deep connection between media agenda and public agenda. Canel, Llamas, and Rev (1996) found a correlation between six topics of public interest and media coverage of these topics. For public interest issues, the findings showed a significant and positive connection between the media agenda and the public agenda. Similarly, Oniebadi (2007) considered the impact of newspapers on the formation of the Kenyan public agenda. Content analysis and surveys were conducted to measure media and public sentiment. The findings support the central hypothesis of agenda setting theory that there is a strong link between the media and the public agenda.

2.7.1.2 Framing and Agenda setting Role of Media

The relationship between the media and the public is very important because people depend on the media for information. The media played an important role in popularizing its agenda by presenting the issues in a specific way. Lal Masjid drew attention in the Pakistani print media supporting the government's cause. These topics are presented in the media in accordance with the government's agenda to influence public opinion in favor of the government (Hossam, Ali et al., 2013). Hameed (2015) explores how Tehreek-e-Taliban Pakistan (TTP) is portrayed in two major media outlets (Jang and Dawn). According to an analysis of the magazine's content, the TTP has been declared a terrorist organization rather than a group of friends. This publication uses an ominous tone to describe them in its news. The media portrayed Pakistan's Tehrik-e-Taliban negatively and sharply criticized their status in Pakistan. In the United States, Pakistan is linked to terrorism and has spread negative stereotypes of Pakistan. Terrorist news often portrays Pakistan in such a way that Pakistan is portrayed and accused of terrorism around the world. On the other hand, after the Zarb-e-Azb operation, the Chinese media projected Pakistan as a victim and a victim of terrorism. The Chinese press has praised Pakistan's security initiatives in the fight against terrorism (Yousaf, 2015).

People presented problems in the same way as the media does, as a result of media framing. Muin (2011) notes that the media places great emphasis on three main topics (weapons of mass destruction, the war in Iraq and the 9/11 attacks) and presents the news in a way that benefits the US government. As a result of this coverage, the public agenda has been set in line with how the topics are presented in their media. When Aubrey and Ahmed (2013) examined how drone strikes were reported in the news, they found that Dawn and The Nation did not provide much publicity for US drone strikes in Waziristan. As a result of this news coverage, people develop negative views, aggression, hostility, and anger toward the US government. Similarly, Dar and Ali (2015) researched the agenda of critical press coverage of drone strikes and found that The New York Times approached the topic positively and presented it in a way that supported their government's goals. On the other hand, the news took a critical stance and gave a negative picture of the situation.

2.7.2 Framing Theory

Framing is a way to present a narrative to your target audience. It involves awareness of reality, highlighting certain interests and ignoring others, creating connections between them. Entman is a character from the movie Entman (2007). Renowned communication scholar Druckman (2001) describes framing as a conflict between "communication frames" or media frames" versus "mental frames or personal frames" in his research studies. According to Scheufele (1999), dichotomy refers to the use of the term framework to describe the process of creating a framework and construction. The framing hypothesis shows that news of a certain problem disseminated by the media has a significant impact on the perception of the problem by viewers. Readers can explore the underlying issues of the topic with a more defined perspective that will influence their perception of politics (Price et al., 1997). Neuman et al. (1992) found that frames are multimedia devices that help to convey information and understand it logically. According to several surveys, when we talk about news footage, we do not believe that it is consistent with the event.

All frameworks have been shown to have the ability to contain for or against a problem or to remain neutral. According to Nisbet (2009), it is not possible to control for the same framework to assess different questions. In addition, the frames can be strong or weak. Compared to competitive tires, their strengths or weaknesses are determined by how well they resonate with their target audience (Chong and Druckman, 2007). Cappella and Jamieson (1997) combined the construction of a new media story with the construction of a new home in their research. Is the creation of a structure in the house as important as in a novelty, so that other elements can be built on it? Since the frame of the house determines its shape, the information frame determines the general background of the event or topic being studied. By comparing Cappella and Jamieson, the press must report the situation in a horrific act, such as terrorism, in order to adhere to the individual decisions that led to radicalization on the one hand, and also to punish the perpetrator on the other. Based on framing theory, this study attempts to configure the pattern and meaning of framing in mainstream media in the light of two important events, as mentioned above.

When making political judgments on an issue, news coverage assists to concentrate the public's attention on certain features of the case and to vary the mix of possible interpretations that a person has. Because this reporting has the capacity to affect people's attitudes, it's crucial to pay attention to the many "frames" (or organizational processes that shape news coverage) accessible in the media in regard to a particular event or group of events. event. According to the researchers, "news preparation" is a process in which "the news media accentuates some parts of social reality while putting others in the background" (Veres, 2005).

People can perceive an issue from various distinct viewpoints, according to framing theory, and these diverse views will impact how a person understands the issue (Vreese, 2012). News frameworks are crucial in political communication because they help to make sense of a series of events and encourage "concrete definitions and interpretations of political problems" by altering the weight or valence of significant aspects in a topic. Citizens will be confronted with many frameworks for the same problem throughout time. when consumers are confronted with news pieces that have been "reframed" It has an impact on not just how political ideas are learnt, but also how they are taught. However, it may cause them to reject rival frames, which may occur later. Repeating a frame of information boosts a person's familiarity or familiarity with it, as well as their capacity to recall it afterwards, according to scientists who research the psychology of the frame effect. Persuasion study shows that repeating a frame leads to agreement with a persuasive message, particularly when the message is unpleasant (De Vries et al., 2003).

According to some public opinion specialists, these elite opinion leaders have a substantial effect on public opinion on political problems, even when the public is ignorant of it. People rely on the elite's point of view to construct their own interpretations of events they don't fully comprehend—and can't. The greater the number of individuals who feel this "elite" is knowledgeable and trustworthy, the more likely their point of view on a topic will be adopted. For a variety of factors, including Pakistan's status as a developing country, Pakistan's political intelligence collecting model must be fundamentally different from that of other countries (Fair, 2014).

Let's start with the reality that Pakistan has a poor information environment since many Pakistanis lack the requisite information-gathering experience. According to data from the Pakistan Social Policy and Development Center (SPDC) in Karachi, the typical Pakistani man obtains 5.5 years of education, compared to only 3.5 years for women (SPDC, 2012). Furthermore, there is a significant disparity in benefits between rural and urban inhabitants. Urban populations aged 15 to 59 had an average of 6.2 years of schooling in 2010-2011, compared to 3.3 years in rural regions. This category of Pakistanis has an average educational performance of 4.28 years.

The productivity gap between rural and urban Pakistanis is much more severe because the bulk of Pakistanis (65%) reside in rural regions. Pakistan is one of the world's most illiterate countries when it comes to literacy rates. It is ranked 180th out of 221 nations evaluated by the (UNESCO). Pakistan has a 55 percent adult literacy rate, with males scoring better (67 percent) than females (42 percent). Reports have been published by the United Nations Educational, Scientific, and Cultural Organization (UNESCO), however Pakistan is a poor country. Pakistan is classified as a lower middle-income country by the World Bank. However, with that number, it is ranked 187th out of 226 nations. According to the statistics, the country's gross national income per capita was $1,275 in 2013. According to media commentators, low circulation of Pakistani newspapers is due to poor literacy, the focus on urban print media, and expensive newspaper pricing (Pakistan Bureau of Statistics, 2015).

Third, Pakistan's infrastructure is inadequate, limiting the access to information available to average Pakistanis. Pakistan has a national electrification rate of 69 percent, compared to 83 percent for all developing nations in Asia and 82 percent for the world average, according to the International Energy Agency's "World Energy Outlook 2014." In Pakistan, there are also considerable disparities in electrification rates between urban and rural regions, with the former having an electrification rate of 88 percent and the latter having a rate of 57 percent (UNESCO, 2014).

These forecasts, however, ignore a phenomenon known as "load discharge," which includes regulated power shutdowns in areas of a power distribution system to prevent system-wide failures when demand exceeds supply. For long years, deferment has been and continues to be a purposeful element of life in Pakistan. People are given early notice about unloading schedules so that they can plan properly. According to a 2013 news article, blackouts last at least 10 hours each day in Pakistani cities.

These projections, however, ignore a phenomenon known as "load shedding," which includes regulated power outages in areas of the power distribution system to avoid system-wide breakdowns when energy demand exceeds supply. For many years, load balancing has been and will continue to be a purposeful part of life in Pakistan. Load shedding schedules are announced in advance so people can plan accordingly. According to a 2013 news report, power outages in Pakistani cities last for at least 10 hours a day.

The average Pakistani person finds it extremely difficult to obtain political information, let alone high quality information, due to the country's human development and ongoing infrastructure problems. Under these circumstances, it is difficult to obtain even simple facts, and the continued secrecy surrounding the US drone program in Pakistan greatly complicates the situation. Officials are reluctant to discuss the program outright because the US government refuses to talk openly about it, and because the program is classified, US officials are forbidden from discussing any specific drone strikes. Various NGOs and press releases from terrorist groups and the Pakistani government provide a lot of information about the programme.

The New America Foundation and the Bureau of Investigative Journalism maintain drone databases based on these press releases, which are widely distributed in the media. These conflicting allegations cannot be verified independently because the drone strikes are restricted to Pakistan's tribal areas, which are governed by the Colonial Frontier Crimes Regulation (FCR). Neither Pakistanis nor foreigners can visit FATA unless they have a personal relationship with a FATA agency, according to the Federal Council. There are many reasons to suspect that the

Pakistani media are covering drone operations, given the significant contribution of the Pakistani military and intelligence services to influencing the Pakistani media (Huma, 2014).

[1] "UN Security Council Resolution 1510 (2003)"

[2] "NATO - Archive ISAF Placemats"

[3] "US Department of Defense, Statement by Acting Defense Secretary Christopher Miller on force levels in Afghanistan, 15 January 2021"

[4] "The US had temporarily deployed additional assets to the region to protect withdrawing forces and civilian contractors, including six B-52 bombers and 12 F-18 fighter aircraft. The Eisenhower carrier strike group also had its deployment to the Arabian Gulf extended. That group was replaced in the North Arabian Sea by the Reagan carrier strike group at the end of June 2021".

[5] "Remarks by President Biden on the drawdown of US forces in Afghanistan, White House, 8 July 2021".

[6] "President Biden, Remarks on the way forward in Afghanistan, 14 April 2021"

[7] "US Department of Defense, Press Briefing, 11 August 2021"

[8] US Department of Defense, Press Briefing, 12 August 2021

[9] "Afghanistan: all foreign troops must leave by deadline – Taliban", BBC News, 5 July 2021

[10] "Department of Defense, Justification for FY2021 Overseas Contingency Operations Afghanistan Security Forces Fund, February 2020"

[11] US Department of Defense, Quarterly Report to Congress, 30 January 2021

[12] ibid

[13] Senate Armed Services Committee, DoD witness statement, 20 May 2021

[14] "General McKenzie Press Availability, US Central Command, 25 July 2021"

[15] "US forces were also based, during the early years of Operation Enduring Freedom at Manas in Kyrgyzstan and Karshi-Khanabad in Uzbekistan. During OEF Tajikistan offered its airspace and military bases for humanitarian purposes".

[16] "Pakistan not to host US forces for Afghan mission", Voice of America, 12 May 2021

[17] "Carrier USS Dwight D. Eisenhower in the Med after 3 months in the Middle East, US Naval Institute News, 6 July 2021"

[18] Statement of the North Atlantic Council, December 2020

[19] North Atlantic Council Ministerial Statement on Afghanistan, 14 April 2021

[20] ibid

[21] "Joint Press Conference of NATO Secretary General and US Secretary of State and US Defense Secretary, 14 April 2021".

[22] "Contributing forces to Resolute Support are set out at: NATO - Archive ISAF Placemats"

[23] "NATO and Afghanistan, 15 April 2021"

[24] "Joint Press Conference of NATO Secretary General and US Secretary of State and US Defense Secretary, 14 April 2021"

[25] "NATO, Resolute Support Mission in Afghanistan, 6 July 2021"

[26] "NATO and Afghanistan, accessed 8 July 2021"

[27] "HC Deb 20 April 2021, c851"

[28] "Ministry of Defense press release, 14 April 2021"

[29] "Liaison Committee, Oral evidence from the Prime Minister, HC491, 7 July 2021, Q.2"

[30] "HC Deb 8 July 2021, c1104"

[31] Ibid.

[32] "HC Deb 20 April 2021, c857"

[33] "HC Deb 20 April 2021, c858"

[34] "HC Deb 8 July 2021, c1114"

[35] "HC Deb 8 July 2021, c1104-5 and c1108"

[36] "Ibid, c1118"

[37] "Afghan President offers three-step peace plan", Voice of America, 30 March 2021

[38] "Mohammed Naeem, Spokesman for the Taliban office in Qatar, 13 April 2021"

[39] "European External Action Service press release, 7 May 2021"

[40] "US State Department press briefing, 11 August 2021".

[41] "Taliban fight on after rejecting Afghanistan power-sharing deal, The Times, 13 August 2021"

[42] "Doha talks on Afghanistan end with call for accelerated peace process, halt to attacks, Reuters, 12 August 2021"

[43] "Joint press conference of Defense Secretary Austin and Chairman of the US Joint Chiefs of Staff, General Mark Milley, 6 May 2021"

[44] "UN Assistance Mission in Afghanistan, 2021 Quarterly Report, April 2021"

[45] "Afghanistan: background and US policy, Congressional Research Service, 21 March 2021"

[46] "House of Lords Select Committee on International Relations and Defence, The UK and Afghanistan, HL208, January 2021. See also The Americans may leave Afghanistan, but the Forever War will grind on, RUSI

Commentary, 16 April 2021"

[47] "Afghan government could collapse six months after US withdrawal, new intelligence assessment says, Wall Street Journalthey"

[48] "Afghanistan: Taliban captures territory as NATO withdrawal continues, Euronews, 5 July 2021"

[49] "In total, nearly 1,600 soldiers are thought to have crossed the border with Tajikistan (BBC News, 6 July 2021)"

[50] "Afghanistan vows to overcome Taliban advances amid US withdrawal, Global Security, 6 July 2021"

[51] ibid

[52] "Afghanistan: briefing ad closed consultations, Security Council Report, 5 August 2021"

[53] "US officials warn collapse of Afghan capital could come sooner than expected", The Washington Post, 11 August 2021

[54] UNHCR, "UNHCR warns of imminent humanitarian crisis in Afghanistan", 13 July 2021

[55]"Office of the UN Human Rights Commissioner, Press Release, 10 August 2021"

[56] "The UK scheme is examined in greater detail in Library Briefing, CBP9286, Resettlement scheme for locally employed civilians in Afghanistan"

[57] "US State Department press briefing, 12 August 2021. See also US Department of Defense press briefing, 12 August 2021"

[58] "US Department of Defense press briefing, 12 August 2021"

[59] "Ministry of Defense press release, 12 August 2021"

[60] ibid

[61] "Afghan leader sees peace talks as dead, braces for civil war", Bloomberg, 9 August 2021

[62] "Afghanistan sees resurgence of warlords, in familiar echo of civil war", Gandhara, 22 April 2021

[63] "Afghanistan: the Taliban seek a negotiated path to power. Will it work? RUSI Commentary, 26 April 2021 and Taliban sets up divide and conquer strategy in Afghanistan, Global Security, 5 May 2021"

[64] Waleed Mir, "Afghanistan's wildcard warlords", The Diplomat, 7 May 2021

[65] "Afghanistan: Hekmatyar ready to join hands with Taliban", Anadolu Agency, 19 September 2020

[66] Waleed Mir, "Afghanistan's wildcard warlords", The Diplomat, 7 May 2021

[67] "Nick Reynolds, The Americans may leave Afghanistan, but the Forever War will grind on, RUSI Commentary, 16 April 2021"

[68] "Nick Reynolds, The Americans may leave Afghanistan, but the Forever War will grind on, RUSI Commentary, 16 April 2021"

[69] "Afghanistan likely headed for civil war", Bloomberg, 8 August 2021

[70] "Russia welcomes the Taliban as a lesser evil in Afghanistan", The Times, 9 August 2021

[71] "US Department of Defense, Press Briefing, 11 August 2021"

[72] "Video supplied by France24, 11 August 2021"

CHAPTER THREE

RESEARCH METHODOLOGY

3.1 Introduction

The methodology aspect of the research is covered in the underlying chapter. Different components and parts of the research methodology have been covered in the supporting chapter. Research methodology aids in the definition and evaluation of processes or strategies that can be utilized to carry out a study in a systematic manner and effectively meet the research objectives. In addition to this research technique basically allows the researcher to configure various strategies or methodologies for assessing the data. Research methodology basically helps the researcher to choose the most efficient and effective methods for a particular research issue. Various aspects of research methodology have been thoroughly covered for this purpose in this chapter of the study, including "research approach, design, philosophy, research instruments, type of investigation, data collection method, sampling, and data analysis techniques, as well as detailed justification and rationale for selecting specific technique". This chapter also includes specific ethical issues that explain the researcher's ethical values when conducting the study.

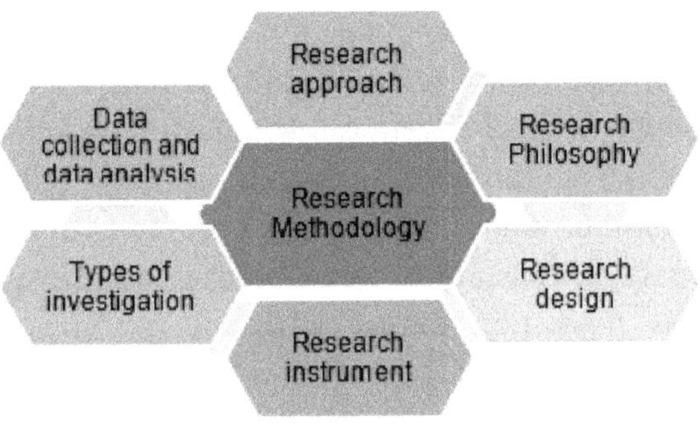

Figure 5 Research methodology

3.2 Research Philosophy

The researcher's research philosophy can be defined as his or her convictions or beliefs about how a given study should be carried out (Kumar, 2019). Philosophy is an important aspect of research since it helps to describe how valuable data may be gathered (Flick, 2015). There are four different styles of research philosophy: pragmatism, Interpretivism, realism, and positivism (Mackey and Gass, 2015). The underlying research philosophy of pragmatism was chosen by the researcher since it provides a diverse range of tools for collecting and analyzing data. Morgan (2014) in his studies stated that the pragmatism philosophy is one wherein researcher can assess the distinct aspects of a research. Hence, it is important on instance where researcher failed to analyze the distinct aspects of a research by a single method. Because it allowed the researcher to cover both the qualitative and quantitative aspects of the study, the pragmatism research philosophy was ideal for the underpinning research.

The reason of choosing the pragmatism research philosophy over Interpretivism is rooted in its importance as it restricts to carry out a research vast range rather than taking into account the interests of a person of the reasons. Whereas positivism research approach is one wherein there is restriction to use any kind of numerical or statistical data. Keeping in view the three approaches researcher identified that the research is incorporating distinct narratives, also it will involve the numerical and statistical data therefore, the pragmatism research philosophy will be more appropriate to choose as it is closer to reality, and it helps a researcher to dig deeper into the reality (Macdonald, 2012). The main benefit of choosing the pragmatic philosophy is its flexible nature by which a researcher can easily choose either a quantitative method, or qualitative method or both on some instance (Goldkuhl, 2012). In this study, the pragmatism research philosophy has been found more appropriate for addressing the research questions and objectives which are based on broad horizons.

3.3 Research Approach

The research approach can be thought of as a strategy that allows authors to conduct the study in a systematic manner while generating acceptable justifications for broad assumptions or hypotheses (Ledford and Gast, 2014). As a result, the three most common research approaches are inductive, abductive, and deductive (Choy, 2014). By pursuing a specific premise to general conclusions approach, inductive research allows for the formulation of a new theory (Kumar, 2019). Abductive research, on the other hand, focuses on modifying existing theories and analyzing incomplete observation patterns by observing the interaction between general and specific data (Gregory and Muntermann, 2011). The deductive approach, on the other hand, promotes the idea of testing hypotheses and theories by following a general assumption to specific conclusion path (Daellenbach and Woiceshyn, 2018).

For the underlying study, researcher choses a deductive technique as this technique was helpful for examining the information and drawing the inferences on the basis of the information generated from the selected sources and events. It also helps to identify the relationship between the selected incidents and newspapers. For this study, it was more suitable to choose the deductive technique as the study has information from general to specific trend which allows the researcher to expand the study results for reaching the final results. Deductive technique is suitable on instance where a researcher wants to check the validity of the data or test the hypothesis of the study as it allows the researcher to explain the data in the light of already existing knowledge and ideas. In case of inductive approach there is large reliance on the observations based on which a researcher creates a theory. However, in doing so a false assumption will cause wrong conclusion whereas a strong assumption will lead to a strong conclusion. Therefore, the deductive approach was found more appropriate for the underlying study.

3.4 Type of Investigation

The three basic types of investigation in any research study were found by Mangal (2013) which incorporate: Explanatory, exploratory and descriptive. When one talk about the exploratory research, it incorporates the one where the basic purpose of a researcher is to examine and discover the already existing concepts (Mackey and Gass, 2015). Similarly, the descriptive research is another form of investigation wherein a researcher tends to explore those areas of information which remain unexplored. Explanatory research in the regard is one wherein a researcher tries to figure out the relationship among the variables of the study and explain them. Through qualitative and quantitative metrics, this study used an explanatory kind of investigation to determine and explain the framing of chosen episodes.

For the underlying study the research design which appeared more suitable was explanatory research as it helps the researcher to identify the impact of one variable on the other on the basis of newly acquired data and information. Studies conducted by Widdowson (2011) postulates that in explanatory research, researcher initially present the study hypothesis in a way by which one can analyze the direction. As the underlying study tends to analyze the coverage of the issues of national and regional importance and their coverage in the two renowned newspapers of the country i.e. Tribune and DAWN, which necessitates the use of explanatory research over descriptive or exploratory research because neither an existing phenomenon nor a novel issue has been investigated. The use of an explanatory research technique can aid in explaining the impact of fluctuations in certain circumstances.

3.5 Research Design

The research design is regarded as one of the most important aspects of research methodology since it determines the nature of the study and the type of data used (Flick, 2015). It also contains a detailed discussion of the research technique used in the study. As a result, the most common study designs are qualitative, quantitative, and mixed method (Macdonald, 2012). To develop analyses and conclusions, the qualitative research paradigm relies on the quality of information and textual sources. The quantitative research paradigm, on the other hand, investigates the underlying processes using numerical and statistical data. On the other hand, mixed-method research incorporates both qualitative and quantitative elements.

The qualitative research paradigm was utilized in the underlying study because it allows researchers to examine both qualitative and quantitative aspects of the study and get extremely precise results. For this objective, the researcher will conduct a content analysis of chosen newspapers. The qualitative paradigm made it easier for the researcher to cover all of the study's topics. Furthermore, qualitative research, according to Rosiek (2013), provides for a more in-depth analysis of data, which assists in the uncovering of hidden patterns related to the issue.

The qualitative aspect of study assist researcher to explain the opinions and justifications in detail that fueled further exploration. The Quantitative paradigm relies on numeric information that helps to incorporate the logical justification for the results. In the underlying study the Qualitative aspect helped the researcher to estimate the extent to which the selected newspapers framed the selected events in selected newspapers. Quantitative reasoning permits to transform the qualitative material or information into statistical data that helps to obtain the results of larger population and considered as more accurate on the basis of statistical calculation (Kumar, 2019). Therefore, it was essential to adopt qualitative method to ensure that all aspects of the study have been covered properly and research problem has been addressed effectively.

3.6 Data Collection Method

The data collecting procedures provide a methodical approach to acquiring information for research from relevant and trustworthy sources (Veal, 2017). The two most often used data collecting methods are primary and secondary data collection. Primary data collection includes information gathered from direct sources such as interviews, focus groups, surveys, and observations (Hair, 2015). Information obtained from existing sources such as journal articles, reports, books, and official online sites is referred to as secondary data collection processes (Ledford and Gast, 2014).

In the underlying investigation, the researcher chose the secondary data collection approach since it allows them to accumulate useful data from firsthand sources that have never been used before in any study. The secondary data collection technique was acceptable for this study since it allowed for the accumulation of current data that was directly relevant to the study's objectives. The researcher used articles from chosen newspapers to acquire critical information about the selected events for this investigation. The researcher's purpose in this study is to look at how the country's leading newspaper has framed national and international events, which demands collecting data directly from relevant sources using a secondary data gathering technique.

3.7 Research Instrument

In this study the content analysis of the archival sections of the Dawn and the Tribune newspaper have been conducted as the research instrument to collect the data from respective sources. So, the research instrument in the given research study is a newspapers i.e. national newspapers of Pakistan (the Dawn and Tribune) based on which the framing analysis has been conducted in the print media of Pakistan regarding the incidents of national and international importance. Therefore, based on the regional importance the Palwama attack leading to 27 February Pak-India escalation and based on the international importance the US withdrawal from Afghanistan has been taken into account. Therefore, the front pages, back pages, national pages and the international pages of these newspapers the Dawn and the Tribune will be analyzed for collecting the relevant information based on the content analysis.

3.8 Data Analysis Technique

Data analysis technique provides the way to examine and investigate the accumulated information systematically (Joffe, 2012). The selection of suitable data analysis technique depends on the type of pf information needs to examine and its sources. The study contemplated by Kumar (2019) advocated that data analysis technique helps to ensure about the reliability and credibility of the data under examination. Particularly, there are different types of technique to analyze both qualitative and quantitative information. In the underpinned study, content analysis technique has been employed by the researcher to evaluate the data gathered through the newspapers. Content analysis helped to formulate different themes based on the data collected and analyses all information under relevant themes. Content analysis was suitable for this study because it permits to simplify the huge and rich data sets easily under encoded themes and facilitates the idea of justifying and validating the collected information with the findings of previous studies.

3.8.1 Content Analysis

Whenever a researcher is interested to conduct a research based on specific concepts of topis in the form of qualitative data it is necessary to conduct the content analysis which is mostly done in text form. By using content analysis method, a researcher can easily measure or evaluate the relation among certain words or themes. Hence in simple words one can define content analysis as a scientific study of the communication in the form of a content. It is absolute study of the various contents of communication and try to assess their meanings and context. It has been regards a most flexible tool for social scientists when the task is to assess the real meanings of the communication prevailed as stated by "Bernard Berelson's publication of Content analysis in Communication Research in 1952". Also, there observed the use of content analysis among certain political scientists and historians as found by Holsti (1968). However, as the social scientists mostly performed qualitative studies therefore, its most prominent use was observed among them (Dominick and Wimmer, 1994:163).

In general terms content analysis is the description of what a communication constitutes, and content is the specific supporting material for carrying out such analysis. It is the process by which a researcher can assess the content of a communication and draw certain inferences and conclusions on the basis of that content as indicated by Nachmias (1976). Furthermore, content analysis straddles the line between observation and document analysis. It is described as an observational approach in the sense that it "takes individual communications and asks questions about communications" rather than asking people to respond to inquiries (Kerlinger, 1973). As a consequence, it's considered a non-intrusive or non-reactive social research technique. "Content analysis is most commonly utilized in social science and mass communication research, while it is used by academics from a variety of fields including social sciences, communications, and psychology, political science, history, and language studies. It has been applied to a wide range of topics, including social change, cultural symbols, changing trends in theoretical content across disciplines, authorship verification, changes in mass media content, nature of news coverage of social issues or problems such as atrocities against women, dowry harassment, social movements, ascertaining propaganda trends, election issues as reflected in mass media content, and so on".

When one wants to analyze journal articles the content analysis approach helps the researcher to investigate the various theoretical patterns and methods for drawing specific conclusions by using the theoretical and methodological patterns (Loy, 1979). When one wants to analyze the newspaper content for the purpose of election coverage the content analysis appeared as a most viable source to shape the opinion of the voter. Studies conducted by Devi Prasad et al. (1991) maintained that the editorial published in the newspapers during election campaigns can be used as the contents for generating themes when one wants to determine the election-related themes. Such themes may be helpful in determining individual voters' perceptions. Trends in the communication content of daily and weekly coverage of development news, political news, and criminal and terrorism news have all been identified using content analysis. Other significant uses of the method included systematic investigations of advertising in newspapers and magazines to draw valuable judgments about country culture and advertiser media preferences (Auter and Moore, 1993; Wang, 1996).

Hence the content analysis is the most prominent technique used by the researcher to develop a qualitative expression of a certain phenomenon i.e., it helps to generalize the data in the form of numbers, percentages and texts which appears more objective. The content analysis techniques is appeared most viable wherein a researcher wants to investigate the research issues of sensitive nature. As the data in such analysis is based on content therefore, the analyzed data has more symbolic meanings. Though it is commonly seen of as a quantitative tool, it may also efficiently capture qualitative material (Stempel, 1989:121). The method's context-sensitivity will be beneficial in defining qualitative characteristics such as the direction of news coverage as positive or negative. In case of data which has some missing information of the data which has been wrongly coded content analysis will be a suitable tool to recheck the data and figure out the prevalent gaps in the text. In case of experimental research or the survey based research the content analysis technique fails to achieve its viable objectives (Woodrum, 1984). It can handle massive amounts of data. Processing is time-consuming, although computers have made it much easier in recent years. It's a low-cost approach that's labor-intensive and doesn't require much in the way of cash. Investigating the data Beginning with a clear explanation of the study's objectives or research questions, content analysis can begin. "What do I want to learn from this communication content?" the researcher asks, laying out the study objectives. As a result, the researcher must select a relevant source of communication and ask questions that can be addressed by content analysis. The purpose of content analysis is to convert "raw" events into data that can be scientifically analysed, allowing for the production of a body of knowledge. In practise, a researcher undertaking a content analysis study must deal with four methodological issues: choosing analysis units, identifying categories, sampling suitable material, and assuring coding reliability (Stempel, 1989).

3.9 Sample Size

For content analysis researcher has selected a respective time frame which was identified as ideal for gathering necessary information. The data from the selected newspaper constitutes the one published by the selected incidents one month before the incident and 1 month when the incidents happened. This information's portray a clear picture of framing and coverage methods adopted by the leading news agencies of the country. Therefore, the content in this regard has been evaluated from the Dawn and the Tribune, where the articles and their first paragraphs has been analyzed. The sample size in this regard is presented below in the given table.

Events	Newspaper	Articles	Total	Date
Palwama	DAWN	93		15 Feb–30 March
	TRIBUNE	99		2019
		192	482	
US Withdrawal	DAWN	167		16 July- 16Sep
	TRIBUNE	123		2021
		290		

Table 1 Sample size

Therefore the table is presenting that the two newspapers, two events and two months' time period for each incident was selected based on which the articles have been obtained which contains the relevant information on the events. So, total 192 articles or contents of Palwama attack leading to 27 February Pak-India escalation (15 February to 30 March 2019) has been obtained where the 93 were published in the Dawn news while 99 were published in the Tribune news. Similarly, total 290 articles or contents of US withdrawal from Afghanistan (6 July- 16Sep 2021) has been obtained where the 167 were published in the Dawn news while 123 were published in the Tribune news. Hence, the total 482 articles has been evaluated and analyzed based on which the framing of print media of Pakistan on the incidents of regional and international importance has been analyzed. In this regard, the topic of interest, sources and frames of these articles in the respective newspapers was analyzed.

For the purpose, the codes was assigned to the given variables for describing the qualitative data into quantitative data into meaningful form based on which the analysis on the SPSS has been conducted for generating the results which is upcoming in the next chapters. The information on these variables is presenting by the given table below.

Variables	Definition	Codes
Newspaper	Dawn	1
	Express Tribune	2
Event Type	Palwama Attack	1
	US Withdrawal from Afghanistan	2
	National Security	1
Topic	International relation	2
	Domestic Politics	3
	Economic Consequence	4
	Other	5

Sources	ISPR	1
	GOP	2
	Reporter/Correspondent/News Desk	3
	News Agencies	4
Independent Variables		
Frame	Episodic	1
	Thematic	2

Table 2 Coding sheet

3.10 Variables

Newspapers, events, topics, sources and frames are the variables in this study which are as follows;

3.10.1 Newspapers

The two newspapers the Dawn and the Tribune have been taken as a sample in this study for analyzing and evaluating the incidents of national and international importance in the print media of Pakistan.

- **The Dawn**

The Dawn Newspaper has been selected for the purpose of investigating the framing of print media of Pakistan. The Dawn is Pakistan's largest and oldest English-language daily, as well as the country's official newspaper (Dawn, 2018). Dawn was launched on October 26, 1941, in Delhi, India, by Quaid-i-Azam Mohammad Ali Jinnah. The journal has offices in Karachi (Sindh), Lahore (Punjab), and Islamabad, as well as correspondents across the world. In this regard the e-paper of the newspaper has been accessed where the archive has been explored for collecting the valuable qualitative data on the Palwama attack leading to 27 February Pak-India escalation and the US withdrawal from Afghanistan. The front page, back page, national and international pages have been evaluated where the articles on these two events were extracted. In this way, research study has collected the 93 articles on Palwama leading to 27 February Pak-India escalation and 167 articles on US withdrawal from Afghanistan. So, the total 260 articles on the two events Pak-India escalation of regional importance and US withdrawal from Afghanistan of international importance have extracted for investigating the framing of print media of Pakistan.

- **The Express Tribune**

The Express Tribune has been chosen as the focus of an investigation of Pakistan's print media framing. The Express Tribune is a Pakistani English-language daily newspaper. It is the Daily Express media group's main publication (Express media group, 2012). In conjunction with International New York Times, the global version of The New York Times, it is Pakistan's sole globally associated newspaper (the express tribune, 2017). Its headquarters are in Karachi, but it also has offices in Lahore, Islamabad, and Peshawar that print copies. It was first published in broadsheet style on April 12, 2010, with a news design that was different from that of typical Pakistani newspapers. In this regard the e-paper of the newspaper has been accessed where the archive has been explored for collecting the valuable qualitative data on the Palwama attack leading to 27 February Pak-India escalation and the US withdrawal from Afghanistan. The front page, back page, national and real mirror pages have been evaluated where the articles on these two events were extracted. In this way, research study has collected the 99 articles on Palwama leading to 27 February Pak-India escalation and 123 articles on US withdrawal from Afghanistan. So, the total 222 articles on the two events Pak-India escalation of regional importance and US withdrawal from Afghanistan of international importance have extracted for investigating the research theme 'framing of the incidents of international and regional importance in the print media of Pakistan: an evidence from Palwama attack leading to 27th February Pak-India escalation and US withdrawal from Afghanistan.

3.10.2 Events

The two events Palwama attack leading to 27 February Pak-India escalation and US withdrawal from Afghanistan, of the regional and international importance, are the samples of this research study, which are as follows;

- **Palwama Attack Leading to 27 February Pak-India Escalation**

The Palwama attacks happened in the Indian-led Kashmir as a result India retaliate and the result was the surgical strikes in Pakistan which Pakistan called a war crime, were two recent events that strained already strained relations (Al Jazeera, 2019). A militant group attacked the Indian army on 14th February 2019 at the area of Palwama, as a result 40 Indian soldiers were killed. India blamed Pakistan for this tragedy. In response Pakistan offered a cooperative investigation of the incidents to find out the real culprit. The offer was rejected by India, and they prepared for the surgical strikes in Pakistan for removing the militant camps (BBC, 2019). On 26th February 2019 there were airstrikes in Pakistan launched by India on a militant hideout, which claims that the airstrike killed a large number of militants (The Hindu, 2019). Whereas Pakistan confirms such airstrikes from India side but they also claimed that there observed no damage as a result of this strike. However, such strikes give rise to the boarder violence among both nations (BBC, 2019). On February 27, 2019, Pakistan sent off airstrikes in Indian-controlled Kashmir. Around the same time, Pakistan destroyed an Indian stream and caught its pilot, Wing Commander Abhinandan Varthaman. Pakistan at first disproved India's case, however later conceded that one of its pilots had disappeared and had been captured by Pakistan (The Hindu, 2019). Therefore, the 27 February 2019 is considered as the day of "Pak-India Escalation" and it was a Palwama attack that resulted into this escalation. In this way, the data or information from the Palwama attack (14Feb 2019) to 27 February Pak-India escalation and till March 2019 has been collected. So, the total number of 192 articles on the Palwama Attack Leading to 27 February Pak-India Escalation has been collected.

- **US Withdrawal from Afghanistan**

With the withdrawal of US and NATO troops from Afghanistan in 2001, a 20-year military campaign was launched to deprive the Taliban of the ability to provide a safe haven for international terrorists, especially Al-Qaeda, and to stabilize the country with a democratic elected government is ending. As the last American soldiers boarded a US military plane on August 31, 2021, terrorists fired rockets at Kabul airport. Members of the democratically elected government including the president escape or hide, and the Taliban gained control of the territory. Most of Afghanistan. Therefore, the 16 August has been considered as the day of "fall of Kabul" when the Taliban has taken the control of the Afghanistan's capital "Kabul". In this way, the data or information before the one month (16 July to 16 Aug) and the data after the one month (16Aug-16Sep) has been obtained on this event. So, the total number of 290 articles on US withdrawal from Afghanistan has been collected.

3.10.3 Topics

The Dawn and the Express Tribune has published the articles on the basis of these topics in their newspapers. So, evaluating these topics, this variable has been designed and coded presented above in the coding sheet table. The topics therefore are as follow.

- National Security
- International Relations
- Domestic Politics
- Economic Consequence
- Other

3.10.4 Sources

- **ISPR**

Inter-Services Public Relations (ISPR) is the media and public relations wing of the Pakistan Armed Forces. It broadcasts and coordinates military news and information for civilian media and civil society in the country. The mission of the ISPR Council is to improve public relations with citizens and civil society through communication with the media. The Palwama attack, which led to a Pak-India escalation on February 27 and the US withdrawal from Afghanistan, were national and international events about which ISPR has issued several warnings.

- **GoP**

The Government of Pakistan, abbreviated as the Government of Pakistan, also known as the Islamic Republic of Pakistan, is a federal government established by the Constitution of Pakistan as the governing body of four provinces, two autonomous regions and one federal territory of a parliamentary democratic republic. The federal, interior, foreign and defense ministries issued comments in response to the Palwama attack and the US withdrawal from Afghanistan was calculated.

- **News Reporters/News Desk/Correspondents**

It deals with the news reporters, correspondents and the news desk of the Dawn and the Tribune news. A correspondent is a journalist who covers a certain region or nation and a specific issue. A reporter is someone who works for a newspaper or a television organization and reports on current events while the news desk is a section of a broadcasting company or newspaper in charge of gathering and reporting news of these newspaper.

- **Agencies**

This source deals with the news of agencies which have been reported by the Dawn and Tribune regarding the Palwama attack leading to 27 February Pak-India escalation and us withdrawal from Afghanistan. The main agencies in this regard were, <u>AGENCY FRANCE PRESS (AFP)</u>, ASSOCIATED PRESS OF PAKISTAN (APP), THE ASSOCIATED PRESS (AP), <u>BRITISH BROADCASTING CORPORATION (BBC)</u>, and REUTERS.

3.10.5 Frame

One of the main objective of the study is to evaluate and analyze the framing of print media of Pakistan. In this regard, the 482 articles have been explored and extracted, for the purpose, the research study is motivated to investigate the framing behind these articles of Palwama and US withdrawal in the Dawn and Tribune. So, episodic and thematic frames has been analyzed from these articles for drawing the inferences on the research theme i.e. Framing of the incidents of international and regional importance in the print media of Pakistan: an evidence from Palwama attack leading to 27th February Pak-India escalation and US withdrawal from Afghanistan.

- **Episodic**

Episodic frame focuses on, individual, single event (event oriented), private realm and considers a problem through life and experience of a particular person. Code 1 has been assigned for the episodic news or contents for the 482 articles that has been published in the Dawn and Tribune for these two events in a given time period.

- **Thematic**

Thematic frame focuses on issue (issues oriented), trends over time, public realm (the surrounding environment, public institutions and considering a problem through government policies, public attitudes etc. Code 2 has been assigned for the thematic news or contents for the 482 articles that has been published in the Dawn and Tribune for these two events in a given time period.

3.11 Ethical Considerations

Ethical considerations are significant aspect of the study that helps author to avoid any sort of ethical misconduct or academic violation. In the underlying study researcher ensure that the data collected from the sources was used under the name of selected source. For this purpose, researcher ensured the information gathered was used purely for academic purposes. Researcher considered the objectivity by selecting the methods and techniques on the basis of their credibility and suitability rather than based on the intuition or self-preferences. Researcher maintained the integrity by incorporating all information in its original form without making any changes, variations or adjustments in data to mold the direction of results. All information obtained from secondary sources has been cited appropriately along with complete bibliography to give the credit to original authors of information and avoid the issues pertaining to academic violation and misconduct. Researcher keenly examine the data and general information to avoid human and typing errors.

CHAPTER FOUR

DATA ANALYSIS AND RESULTS

4.1 Introduction

This chapter is dealing with the data analysis and results which have been collected for the content analysis in order to investigate the research questions, objectives, and hypotheses of underpinned study. For the purpose, the qualitative data has been thoroughly analyzed, evaluated and obtained where it was converted into quantitative data for analyzing on SPSS statistical software for generating the inferences on the research theme. Therefore, two newspapers i.e., the Express TRIBUNE and DAWN has been selected where the framing of events of international and national importance have been assessed for determining the coverage of Pakistan's print media on such instances. The selected events were US withdrawal and PALWAMA attack leading to 27th February Pak-India escalation from where data has been extracted before and after the one months of the incidents.

4.2 Results and Discussion

It is pertinent to mention here that one of the significant objectives of the study was to ascertain the framing of print media of Pakistan. For the reason, the two events, two newspapers and two months, one each before and after the events have been selected which are elaborated in the underlying table:

Newspapers		Events		Time Period	
DAWN	TRIBUNE	US Withdrawal	Palwama Attack	1 Month Before	1 Month After

The table is depicting that the two selected newspapers were DAWN and TRIBUNE, both have a significant role in framing the major events of both national and international importance. Along with this the two prescribed events i.e.., US Withdrawal and Palwama attack were observed in the dailies of the selected newspapers. As it was not possible to cover the whole incidents therefore, researcher set a time period for observing the news coverage in the selected newspaper. The time period observed was 1 month before the occurrence of selected events and one month after the occurrence of selected events. For observing the events first page, second page, national and international sections of both newspapers have been explored on the topics of national security, international relations, domestic politics, economic consequence and others under the sources of ISPR (Inter Services Public Relations), GoP (Government of Pakistan), news desk/reporters/correspondents and agencies (AFP, AP, Reuters and other). Two types of frames were generated during the data collection from respective sources. One frame was episodic which focuses on a single issue and observed it in episodes while the other was the thematic frame which focuses to observe the trends associated with that issue over a time. The articles on the Palwama attack leading to 27th February Pak-India escalation have been selected from 15 February to 30 March 2019 and articles on the US withdrawal from Afghanistan has been collected from the time period of 16 July to 16 September, 2021 respectively.

4.2.1 Coding of Data

After identifying the frames, time period and the sources the next stage was data coding. The coding was designed for the purpose of data collection based on which inferences were drawn on the underpinned study. For coding some specific numerical values were assigned to the selected events, newspapers, topics under which the issues were assessed and the sources by which the newspapers got news of the events and then cover those. Hence the numerical values assigned for the coding purpose can be viewed from the given table;

Newspaper	C	Event Type	C	Topic	C	Sources	C	Frame	C
DAWN	1	PALWAMA	1	National Security	1	ISPR	1	Episodic	1
TRIBUNE	2	US Withdrawal	2	International Relations	2	GoP	2	Thematic	2
				Domestic Politics	3	News Reporter	3		
				Economic Consequence	4	Agencies	4		
				Other	5				

Table 3 Coding data

On the basis of above table one can observe the codes which are presenting the occurrence of newspapers, events, topics, sources and frames where code 1 was assigned for DAWN newspaper while code 2 was assigned for TRIBUNE newspaper of this category. Similarly, for the variable event 1 was assigned for PALWAMA and code 2 was assigned for US Withdrawal. Meanwhile, for assessing the next variable which was the topic under which the selected news were published coding has been done where 1 was assigned for representing national security, 2 for international relations, 3 for domestic politics, 4 for economic consequence and 5 for the other. Furthermore, in the variable sources, 1 was assigned for ISPR, 2 for GoP, 3 for reporters and 4 for agencies. At the end for forecasting the framing variable of the study i.e., frame the above table depicts the code 1 for episodic and 2 for thematic frames.

4.2.2 Data Extraction

After identifying the codes for respective data the next process was the data extraction. For data extraction researcher thoroughly do a content analysis of selected newspapers for selected events in the said time period. The table below in this regard is presenting the number of articles extracted on the respective events from the selected newspapers for the given period of time.

Newspaper	Event		Total
	Palwama	US Withdrawal	
DAWN	93	167	260
TRIBUNE	99	123	222
Total	192	290	482

Table 4 Number of Articles

The table is presenting the number of articles extracted on Palwama attack and US withdrawal from Afghanistan. From the figure presented above once can analyze that Dawn has published the 260 articles in total, out of which 93 were on the Palwama incident and the rest of 167 on the US withdrawal while Tribune has published the 222 articles in total, out of which 99 were on the Palwama and 123 were on the US withdrawal. Therefore, the total 192 articles on the Palwama attack and 290 articles on the US withdrawal has been obtained in this study where the 260 articles on both events were extracted from the Dawn Newspaper and 222 from the Express Tribune. The data collected from was used for generating the conclusion based on which the researcher address the research questions and objectives of the study. The graphical presentation of above table is given as follow:

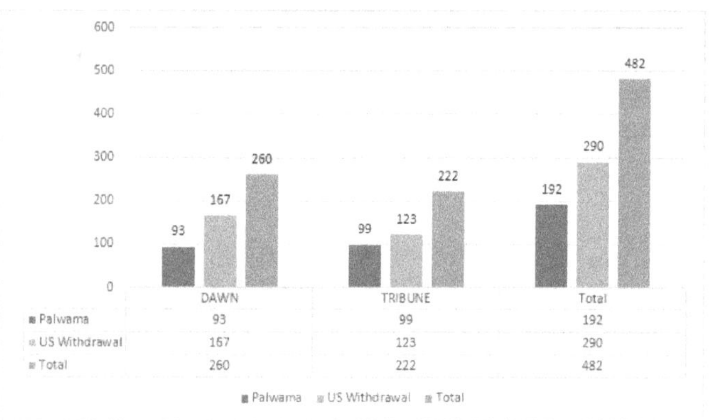

Figure 6 Number of articles

4.2.3 *Combined Analysis of the Extracted Data*

After observing overall extracted data there observed the need for assessing the distribution of the data. For the purpose the frequencies and percentages of the extracted data were assessed which helps the researcher to observe the percentage of data sources and the number of time of events occurrence. It was useful for observing the weightage given by respective newspapers to the selected event. In this regard the table below is presenting the newspapers, events, topics, sources, and frames of these news or articles where the frequencies and percentages are given.

Newspaper

	Frequency	Percent	Valid Percent	Cumulative Percent
DAWN	260	53.9	53.9	53.9
Express TRIBUNE	222	46.1	46.1	100
Total	482	100	100	

Event

	Frequency	Percent	Valid Percent	Cumulative Percent
PALWAMA	192	39.8	39.8	39.8
US WITHDRAWL	290	60.2	60.2	100
Total	482	100	100	

Topic

	Frequency	Percent	Valid Percent	Cumulative Percent

National Security	61	12.7	12.7	12.7
International Relations	374	77.6	77.6	90.2
Domestic Politics	4	0.8	0.8	91.1
Economic Consequence	9	1.9	1.9	92.9
Other	34	7.1	7.1	100
Total	482	100	100	

Source

	Frequency	Percent	Valid Percent	Cumulative Percent
ISPR	26	5.4	5.4	5.4
GOP	90	18.7	18.7	24.1
News Reporter/News Desk/Correspondent	162	33.6	33.6	57.7
Agencies/Reuters	204	42.3	42.3	100
Total	482	100	100	

Frame

	Frequency	Percent	Valid Percent	Cumulative Percent
Episodic	123	25.5	25.5	25.5

Thematic	359	74.5	74.5	100
Total	482	100	100	

Table 5 Analysis of Combined data

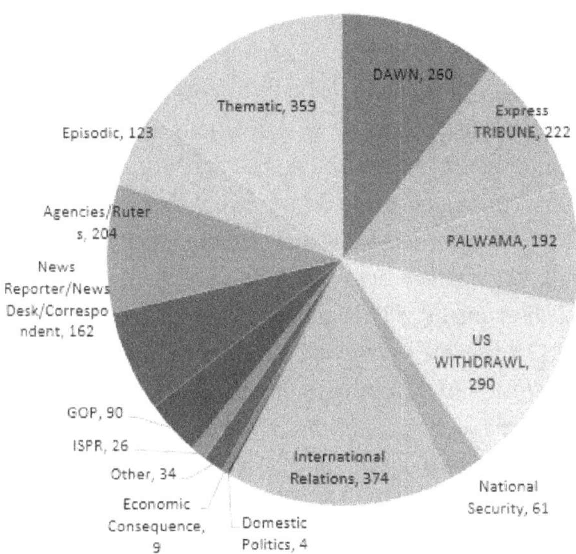

The table is presenting the statistics which have been analyzed on the SPSS regarding the information extracted from the 2 newspapers for selected events and during the selected time period of two months for evaluating and analyzing the research questions. In this regard, the table depicts that 482 total articles from two newspapers on the two events (Palwama and US withdrawal) have been analyzed i.e. 260 articles were analyzed from the DAWN news on Palwama and US withdrawal whereas 222 articles were analyzed from the express Tribune on these two events. Therefore, it is concluded that Dawn has reported the 260 articles on both events and Tribune has reported the 222 articles on the Palwama and US withdrawal for 2 months

before and after the incidents. Furthermore, it has also been investigated that out of 482 articles, 192 articles were reported on Palwama attack leading to Pak-India escalation while 290 articles were reported on US withdrawal from Afghanistan in the two given newspaper. Moreover, pie chart on the basis of SPSS analysis further depicts that 374 news were on the topic of international relations, 61 were on the national security, 4 were on domestic politics, 9 on the economic consequence and 34 were published on the other topics. In this way, it has been observed that agencies were the source of 204 articles, news reporters were the source of 162 articles, government of Pakistan was the source of 90 articles and ISPR was the source of 26 articles. At the end, it is analyzed that 359 frames were thematic and 123 frames in both newspapers was episodic. Therefore, in this regard, researcher has analyzed the framing of print media of Pakistan i.e. the DAWN and TRIBUNE, where the total number of articles, topics and frames have been analyzed. The percentages in this regard are present below in the column graph.

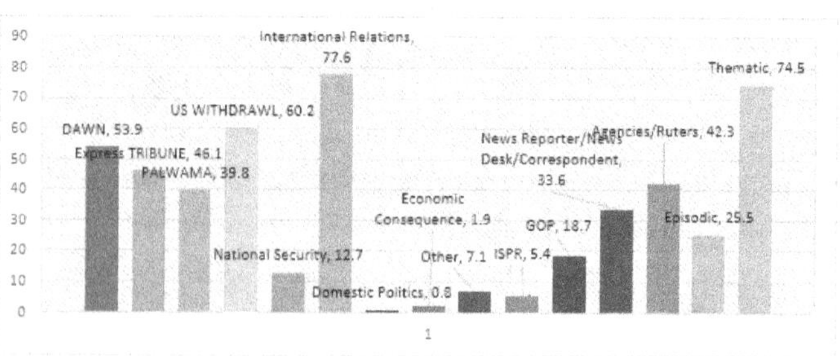

Figure 7 Graphical presentation of combined data

The graph is presenting the percentages of framing of two events (Palwama and US withdrawal) in two newspapers (Dawn and Tribune) for two months in Pakistan, based on which it is concluded that both newspapers have reported the 482 articles on these two events where the percentage of Dawn newspaper was 60 percent while Tribune was 46 percent. Which presents that in the dailies of Dawn newspaper the selected events gained much hype as compare to those in Tribune. Similarly, the event of Palwama has gain the coverage of 40 percent in both newspapers while the event US withdrawal has gain the coverage of 60 percent, respectively which presents that more coverage was given to the incidence of international importance.

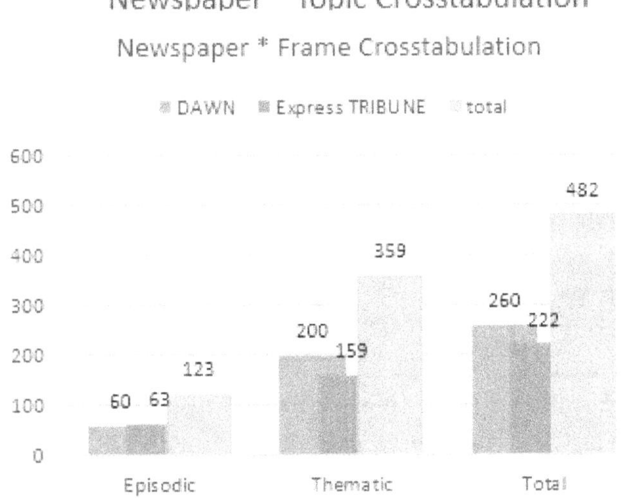

Additionally, it was observed that 78 percent of coverage has been given to the topic of international relations on both events in both newspapers, 13 percent has given to national security, 1 percent has given to domestic politics, 2 percent has given to economic consequences and 7 percent has given to other topics. In this way, the 74.5 percent frames were thematic and 25.5 were episodic where the 42 percent of the sources were the agencies, 34 percent were the news reporters, 19 percent was the government of Pakistan and 5 percent of the source was ISPR in Dawn and Tribune on the Palwama attack and US withdrawal during the two months. In general, the researcher comes to know that both newspapers interestingly portray the events while the events of international importance gained much hype as compare to national and in Dawn dailies and has put more emphasis on the coverage of both events as compared to Tribune as depicting in the bar graph. Furthermore, it is also evaluated that the Dawn has emphasized more on the thematic framing i.e. out of 260 articles on Palwama and US withdrawal, 23% (60 articles) coverage was conducted on episodic framing while 77% (260 articles) of coverage has been taken onto thematic framing on both events. Whereas, the Tribune has covered the 28% (63 articles) on episodic framing and 71% (159artcieles) on the thematic framing on Palwama and US withdrawal out of its 222 articles. Therefore, both newspapers had given the 25.5% (123 articles) coverage on episodic framing and 74.5% (359 articles) coverage to thematic framing as depicting by the c

4.2.4 Descriptive Statistics

Descriptive statistics describes the essential characteristics of the data utilized in the investigation. The objective of descriptive statistics, also known as summary statistics, is to summarize quantitative data in an understandable way, according to William (2006). In addition, summary statistics for the study model were calculated using SPSS in order to simplify the bigger data and demonstrate its key aspects in order to present the research study. In this case, the quantitative data analysis was employed by the researcher to analyses and evaluate the study subject, i.e. framing of international and regional events in Pakistani print media: evidence from the Palwama attack, which led to a Pak-India escalation on February 27th and the US pullout from Afghanistan. Because descriptive statistics serve as the foundation for future research, such as inferential analysis, it aids readers in the replication of studies. As a result, summary statistics' goal is to show variability or central tendency, as well as to convey the meaning of regressed data to readers through tables, graphs, and general remarks. In this way, the mean, or central tendency, describes the entire collection of data, which is truly essential to the entire set. Meanwhile, it depicts the distribution's center location for the provided set of data. The standard deviation is a measure of dispersion that shows how a data collection deviates from the mean value. The larger the standard deviation, the wider the dispersion from the mean, and the smaller the number, the closer the data points are to their mean. A high standard deviation indicates that the data points are distributed throughout a larger range of values, whereas a low standard deviation indicates that the data points are close to the mean. As a result, the summary statistics are described in the table below. These statistics are used to display the behavior of the sample data's many variables. Various factors were assessed from a larger collection of data in the current research investigation. As a result, descriptive statistics were created to break down this larger quantity of data into a more manageable format. According to Sharma (2019), descriptive statistics may be used to break down large amounts of data into the simplest possible form, such as presenting the average of each action in a clear and understandable manner. As a result, the table below shows the mean, variance, standard deviation, Skewness, and kurtosis of the variables that were investigated during the underlying research study.

Descriptive Statistics

	N	Minimum	Maximum	Mean	Std. Deviation	Variance	Skewness		Kurtosis	
	Statistic	Statistic	Statistic	Statistic	Statistic	Statistic	Statistic	Std. Error	Statistic	Std. Error
Newspaper	482	1.00	2.00	1.46	.49	.24	.15	.11	-1.98	.22
Event	482	1.00	2.00	1.60	.49	.24	-.41	.11	-1.83	.22
Topic	482	1.00	5.00	2.13	.91	.82	2.14	.11	4.68	.22
Source	482	1.00	4.00	3.12	.90	.81	-.70	.11	-.46	.22
Frame	482	1.00	2.00	1.74	.43	.19	-1.12	.11	-.73	.22

Table 6 Descriptive statistics

4.3 Palwama Attack

For analyzing the framing of the incidents of international and regional importance in print media of Pakistan, Palwama attack leading to 27th February Pak-India Escalation has been taken into account as it has the regional as well as international role and importance in Pakistan. Based on which the Palwama attack has been evaluated and analyzed in the two national English newspapers of Pakistan i.e. the Dawn and the Tribune. The main motive of selecting these newspapers was to assess the framing of print media of Pakistan in the leading newspapers of the country. For the purpose, the articles on Palwama attack has been explored in the front, back, national and international sections of these two newspapers where the 192 articles were extracted. This data has then coded and analyzed on the SPSS for generating the results on the research questions and objectives of the study. So, in this regard the analysis on these 192 articles on Palwama attack leading to 27 February Pak-India escalation in the print media of Pakistan (Dawn and Tribune) are as follows.

Newspaper		Topic					Frame		Total
DAWN	Express TRIBUNE	NS	IR	DP	EC	Other	Episodic	Thematic	
93	99	48	134	4	1	5	69	123	192

Table 7 Palwama attack framing statistics

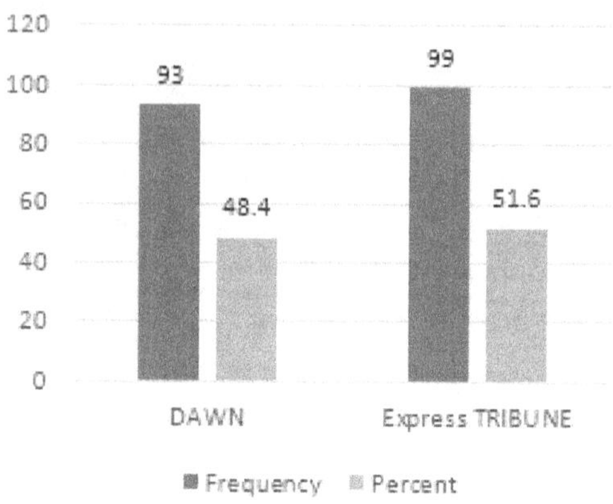

Figure 8 Articles on Palwama in Dawn and Tribune

The table is presenting the data analysis on the 192
articles regarding the Palwama attack in the print media of
Pakistan (Dawn and Tribune) for the period 15 February
2019 – 30 March 2019 where it is presenting that Dawn
has reported the 93 articles on Palwama attack and Tribune
has reported the 99 articles on Palwama attack leading to
27 February Pak-India escalation. Therefore, it is concluded
that Dawn has given the 48 percent coverage to Palwama
attack for the said period (15feburary-30March) while
Tribune has given the 52 percent coverage to Palwama
attack leading to 27 February Pak-India escalation in the
given time period. This suggests that the Tribune has given
more coverage to the issue of national importance as
compared to Dawn.

4.3.1 *Topics under which Palwama attack was framed*

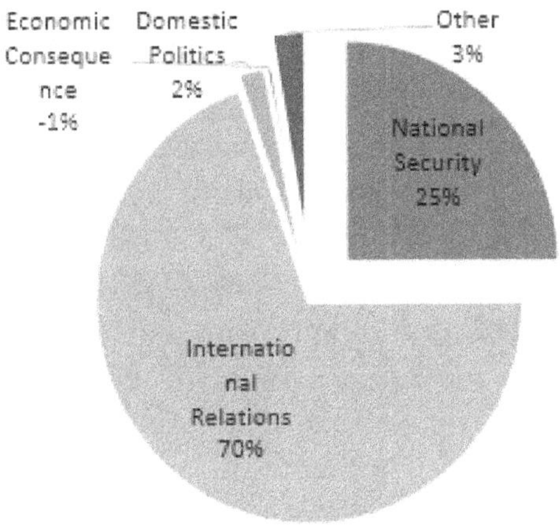

Enter Caption*Figure 9 Topics under which Palwama attack was framed*

In any newspaper topics always remain under the main consideration. By topic we mean the special scenarios under which a particular newspaper analyzed a particular event. As here our main focus is on Palwama Attack therefore, this section will assess how the Palwama was assessed as a topic of national security i.e., one causing the threats to the security of nation, as well as how it is affecting the international relations of our country with its neighbor. The third topic under which the issue was addressed was relevant to the domestic politics where the role of national political leaders towards the issue were assessed. The next topic was economic consequence where the impact of issue on the economy was assessed. Along with this some other topics were also assessed on the basis of information obtained from these newspapers. The results are present in the graph. The graph is depicting the statistics on the variable of topic i.e. under which topics the Dawn and Tribune has frame the 192 articles on Palwama attack. Based on which it is analyzed that Dawn and Tribune has frame the 48 articles which were of the importance of national security on Palwama attack in their newspapers. Similarly, 134 articles were on the importance of international relations, 4 were on the domestic politics, 1 on the economic consequence while 5 on the other relevant topics. Therefore, it is concluded that Dawn and the Tribune has published the total 192 articles on Palwama attack for the period 15feb-30march 2019 where 25 percent articles were on national security, 70 percent on international relations, 2 percent on domestic politics, .5 percent on the economic consequences while 2.6 percent on the other topics.

4.3.2 Sources of news on Palwama Attack

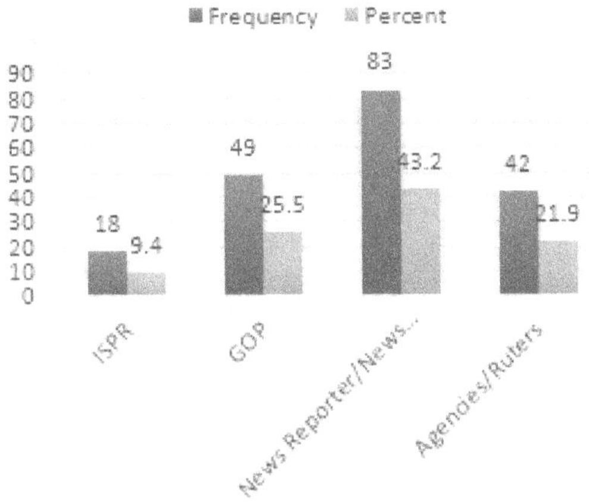

Figure 10 Sources of news on Palwama Attack

Enter Caption*Figure 10 Sources of news on Palwama Attack*

By a news source we mean the way by which these newspapers get the information of the incident. As the incident occurs outside the boundaries of the country so it was not possible for newspaper to directly approach the site of incident and to collect information. There are various sources by which newspapers do coverage of a certain incident. This section will address the sources by which Palwama attack was framed in the selected newspapers.

The sources which were analyzed during this study can be observed from the given graph which states that out of 192 articles on Palwama attack (Dawn, 93 and Tribune, 99) the source of 22 percent (42news) were agencies, the source of 43 percent (83 news) was desk/reporters/correspondents, the source of 25.5 percent (49 news) was government of Pakistan, while ISPR was the source of 9 percent (18) news in Dawn and Tribune newspapers on the Palwama attack for the period 15Feb-30Mar 2019.

4.3.3 Types of Frames identified during Palwama Attack

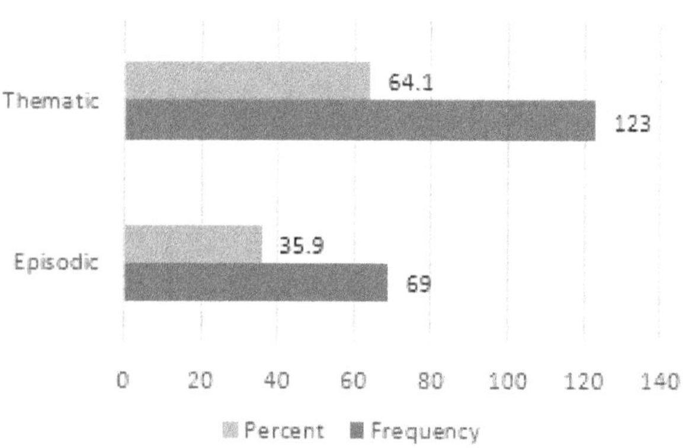

Enter Caption*Figure 11 Types of Frames identified during Palwama Attack*

There are two types of frames as mentioned before i.e., episodic and thematic. The frames identified during the data collection of Palwama attack is given in the given graph. The graph presents that the episodic and thematic news was investigated in order to analyze the framing analysis of the print media regarding the event. The outcomes generated on SPSS on the collected data is as depicted in the graph where it was observed that 123 (64 percent) articles were the thematic while 69 (36) percent of the articles were the episodic which is more clearly depicting in the column graph as well. So it is concluded that the most of the news in the print media of Pakistan were the thematic news on Palwama attack leading to 27 February Pak-India escalation.

4.4 US Withdrawal

As the other issue asses was US withdrawal from Afghanistan. In response the framing was assessed in the light of both newspapers. For analyzing the framing of the incidents of international importance in print media of Pakistan, US withdrawal has been taken into account as it has the regional as well as international role and importance in Pakistan. Therefore, the US withdrawal has been evaluated and analyzed in the two national English newspapers of Pakistan i.e. the Dawn and the Tribune. For the purpose, the articles on US withdrawal from Afghanistan has been explored in the front, back, national and international sections of these two newspapers where the 290 articles were extracted. This data has then coded and analyzed on the SPSS for generating the results on the research questions and objectives of the study. So, in this regard the analysis on these 290 articles on US withdrawal from Afghanistan in the print media of Pakistan (Dawn and Tribune) are as follows.

Newspaper		Topic				Frame		Total
DAWN	Express TRIBUNE	NS	IR	EC	Other	Episodic	Thematic	
167	123	13	240	8	29	54	236	290

Table 8 US withdrawal framing statistics

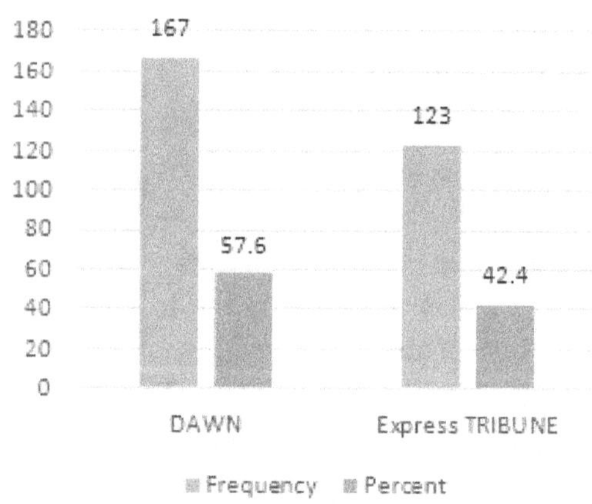

*Figure 12 Articles on US withdrawal in the Dawn and
Tribune*

The table is presenting the data analysis on the 290
articles regarding the US withdrawal from Afghanistan in
the print media of Pakistan (Dawn and Tribune) for the
period 16 July 2021 - 16 Sep 2021 where it is analyzed that
Dawn has reported the 167 articles on US withdrawal and

Tribune has reported the 123 articles on US withdrawal from Afghanistan, as depicting in the column graph. Therefore, it is concluded that Dawn has given the 57.6 percent coverage to US withdrawal from Afghanistan for the period (16July-16Sep) while Tribune has given the 42.4 percent coverage to US withdrawal from Afghanistan for the period (16July-16Sep).

4.4.1 Topics under which US withdrawal was framed

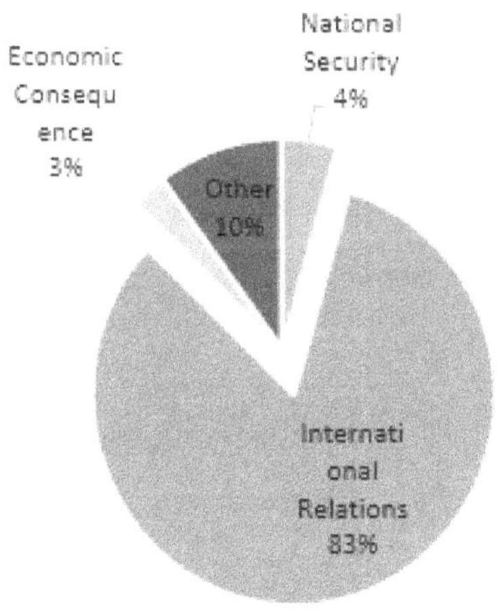

Enter Caption*Figure 13 Topics under which US withdrawal was framed*

The graph is depicting the statistics on the variable of topic i.e. under which topics the Dawn and Tribune has published the 290 articles on US withdrawal in their newspapers where it is presenting that Dawn has reported the 167 articles on US withdrawal and Tribune has reported the 123 articles on US withdrawal from Afghanistan based on the given topics. Therefore, it is concluded that Dawn and the Tribune has published the 13 (4.5) articles on US withdrawal from Afghanistan on the topic of national security of Pakistan, 240 (82 percent) of articles on the topic of international relations, 8 (3 percent) articles were on the topic of economic consequence while 29 (10 percent) articles on US withdrawal was on the other topics for the period 16July2021-16Sep2021.

4.4.2 Sources of news on US withdrawal

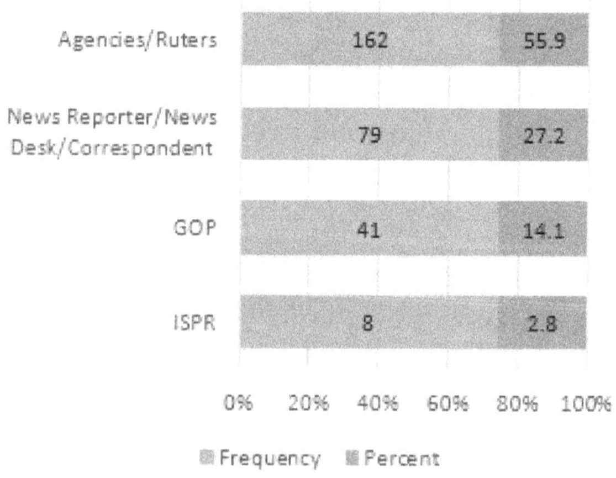

Figure 14 Sources of news on US withdrawal

Furthermore, out of 290 articles on US withdrawal from Afghanistan in (Dawn, 167 and Tribune, 123) the source of 60 percent (162news) was agencies, the source of 27 percent (79 news) was news desk/reporters/

correspondents, the source of 14 percent (90 news) was government of Pakistan, while ISPR was the source of 2.8 percent news. Therefore, the framing of these news or articles i.e. 290 (Dawn 167 and Tribune 123) on US withdrawal from Afghanistan has been analyzed where the episodic and thematic news was investigated in order to analyze the framing analysis of the print media regarding the events of regional and international importance. The outcomes generated on SPSS on the collected data is as follows;

4.4.3 *Types of Frames identified US Withdrawal*

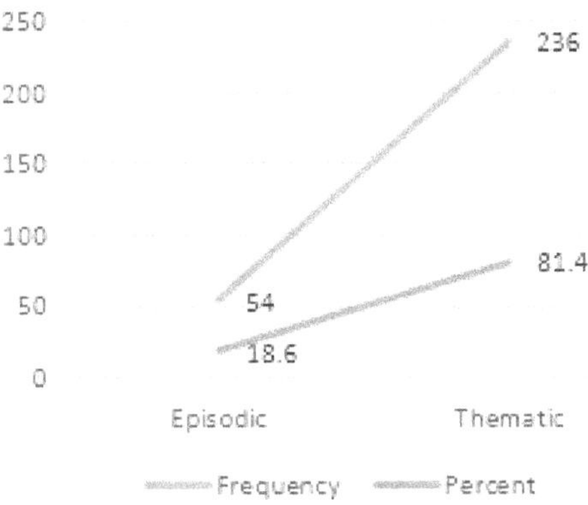

Figure 15 Types of Frames identified US withdrawal

The graph is presenting the outcomes on the thematic and episodic framing behind the 290 articles in both newspapers regarding the US withdrawal from Afghanistan. So, it is depicting the out of 290 articles from

16th July 2021 to 16th September, 2021 on US withdrawal from Afghanistan the 236 (81.4 percent) of frames were the thematic while 54 (18.6) percent of the frames were the episodic. So, it is concluded that the most of the news in the print media of Pakistan was the thematic frames on US withdrawal from Afghanistan.

CHAPTER FIVE

CONCLUSION AND RECOMMENDATIONS

It is a well-known reality in modern society that people look to various sources of information, such as print media, social media, or other for staying informed about what is going on in the world, particularly in topics of national and international politics, security, and events such as wars and conflicts. As a result, a robust mass media is required to keep people informed about global political and social events. Different social, political, economic, and cultural ideals and institutions impact the media sector or they get influenced by the mainstream media. According to literature, the media sector is under the influence of institutions with political, cultural, and economic clout. Theoretically, the informative content on media outputs is sometimes ideologically molded. The goal of this ideologically motivated information is to replicate and enhance oppressive and exploitative social connections. Furthermore, media ideological constructs are naturalized, and the public interprets media "information" as part of their "common sense" knowledge. As a result, it has been established that, because media may be controlled by many organizations in society, it can never be considered to reflect "reality," but just "representations of reality."

Framing effects, according to several studies, are always the result of widespread public exposure to mass media since it has the capacity to change our ideas about certain issues and events. Individuals are largely reliant on the media for information, according to various studies, and it has a substantial impact on molding their viewpoints on the conflicts about which they acquire information from the media. Furthermore, some analysts see the media as a two-edged sword with the power to both transmit and deescalate tensions throughout the world. This type of media conflict may be simply identified by framing in the light of media. Pakistan's media is praised for its outspoken independence on occasion; nonetheless, the country's media engages in substantial self-censorship and goes to great pains to appease the military and intelligence services. Through massive advertising and public awareness expenditures, the Pakistani government maintains a strong grip on the media. The government also has an influence on daily life by restricting paper supply and selectively enforcing restrictions.

For a democracy to thrive, it is necessary to have a free press. It assists people in gathering knowledge that might otherwise be difficult to obtain. Furthermore, free media frequently works as a vigilant watchdog for the people of any country. When it comes to the relationship between mass media and ideology, it is widely acknowledged that media has the ability to control the public. Different media organizations promote "false consciousness" among viewers in order to support the vested interests of a society's "specialized elite." After the parliament, government, and judiciary, the media is recognized as the fourth pillar of the state in Pakistan. Furthermore, the freedom to information is strongly safeguarded by Pakistan's constitution, which acts as a legal framework for Pakistani media and prohibits anything that is contrary to Islam, Pakistan's security, or morals. We can notice a lot of changes in Pakistan's political and social situation right now.

Pakistan is a crucial player in the global fight against terrorism, but it also has a number of internal disputes. Similarly, the Pakistani media is frequently accused by various segments of society of spreading incorrect information to the general public. In this regard, the general public believes that they were frequently confused, resulting in a lack of decision-making and initiative. Due to the strategic relevance, fragile pluralistic characteristics, and delicate diplomatic connections, it has also been discovered that keeping many events or news as a secret record on behalf of competent organizations has become a tendency. Print media, on the other hand, is tasked by the constitution with the right to free expression, and as a result, it has evolved as a fourth pillar of the state. In this regard, the current research study attempts to look into the framing of national and international events in Pakistan's print media.

The current study aims to uncover the involved ideological structures in Pakistani print media, with a particular focus on the Dawn and Express Tribune media groups, by examining the Palwama incident, which resulted in a Pak-India escalation on February 27 and the US pullout from Afghanistan. In this approach, the researcher looked at the Dawn and Tribune newspapers from 15 February to 30 March 2019 and 16 July to 16 September 2021 to form conclusions about the Palwama and US pullout occurrences of national and international significance. The objectives of the present study were to review the importance of issue in the print media by understand the framing analysis of print media of Pakistan with special emphasis to Dawn and Tribune media groups. So, study is examined that how the incidents of national and international relevance are framed in Pakistan's print media where it evaluated and analyzed the framing of Palwama attack leading to 27 February Pak-India Escalation and US withdrawal from Afghanistan in the Dawn and Tribune newspapers. Furthermore, the study analyzed the topics, sources and frames based on which the print media (the Dawn and Tribune) has reported the incidents (Palwama and US withdrawal). In this way, the research study has analyzed the credibility of Pakistan's print media in framing the incidents of national and international importance.

It is pertinent to describe that the Dawn and Express Tribune has been assessed for analyzing the framing of print media of Pakistan in relation to the events of national and international importance. For the purpose, the two events i.e. Palwama attack leading to 27 February Pak-India escalation and the US withdrawal from Afghanistan and the two newspapers i.e., Dawn and Tribune have been examined where the 482 articles have been extracted. In this way the research study has investigated these two objectives i.e., to understand the framing analysis of print media of Pakistan with special emphasis to Dawn and Tribune media groups and examine how the incidents of national and international relevance are framed in Pakistan's print media.

Based on these two research objectives, study concludes that the Dawn and Tribune has published the 482 articles on Palwama attack and US withdrawal from Afghanistan. In this way, it is analyzed that Dawn has published the

260 articles, 93 on the Palwama incident and the 167 on the US withdrawal while Tribune has published the 222 articles, 99 on the Palwama and 123 on the US withdrawal. Therefore, 192 articles or news (93 Dawn, 99 Tribune) was published on the Palwama attack leading to 27 February Pak-India escalation and 290 articles or news (167 Dawn, 123 Tribune) has been published on the US withdrawal from Afghanistan.

So, the 482 articles from newspapers (Dawn 260, Tribune 222) on the events (Palwama 192, US withdrawal 290) in the time period (15 Feb-30 March, 2019 and 16 Jul-16 Sep, 2021) has been evaluated and analyzed where it is found that the 74.5 percent of frames were thematic while 25.5 percent frames was the episodic. Moreover, these newspapers have framed the Palwama and US withdrawal on the basis of 77 percent of international relations, 13 percent of national security, 1 percent of domestic politics, 2 percent of economic and 7 percent of other frames. It is also concludes that 42 percent of the sources was agencies, 34 percent was news reporters/correspondents, 19 percent was government of Pakistan and 5 percent was ISPR. So, in this way researcher has investigated the objectives of the study and analyzed the framing of print media of Pakistan "the Dawn and Tribune" on the incidents of national and international importance "the Palwama attack leading to 27 February Pak-India escalation and US withdrawal from Afghanistan". Therefore, it is concluded that Dawn and Tribune has given the ample importance to these events where they have published the articles based on multiple sources and topics. Hence, it is concluded that the print media of Pakistan has published the average 3-4 articles on their dailies regarding these events of national and international importance where the national security (war and terror) frame, international relations frame, political, social, economic and other frames were approached. The different ministries of the government like interior, foreign and defense have been framed regarding their perceptions on these events. So, the objective of the study to analyze the topics, sources and frames based on which the print media (the Dawn and Tribune) has reported the incidents (Palwama and US withdrawal) has been full filled. One other thing revealing about this fact is that researcher had included only those articles which contains the message of these incidents in their statement or first paragraph while the other has been deducted from the data. For a more detailed analysis of these two events, researchers discovered that the Tribune published more stories on Palwama, which is a national-level occurrence, while the Dawn published more stories on the US pullout, which is a global-level incident. Dawn News, on the other hand, focused more on thematic framing and showed more genuine sources, whilst Tribune concentrated more on its news desk. It was observed that the news coverage by Dawn was different from that of Tribune particularly in addressing the national security, the economic consequences, and international relations. As a result of the foregoing debate, it is believed that the study looked into its research questions that how the Dawn and Tribune portrayed the Palwama incident, which led to a Pak-India escalation on February 27 and the US withdrawal from Afghanistan.

As a fourth pillar of the state in Pakistan, the media has the ability to diffuse tensions and intolerance in all sectors of society. The media authorities in Pakistan have a societal obligation to contribute to social peace and stability in the country by playing a beneficial role. As a result, it is envisaged that through self-regulating their own media networks, Pakistan's media authorities would seek to promote tolerance, harmony, peace, and stability. In a fast-paced Pakistani society, the news media plays a vital role. Since the beginning of the information revolution, there has been an increase in the use of news media for diverse purposes. However, it has been acknowledged as a major component in the development of opinions from its origin. The presence of a news media in a culture has a considerable impact on how the general public perceives the world. Individuals are exposed to current events on a national and worldwide level through news media, which allows them to express their opinions. In today's world, the media is unquestionably a weapon of war. This is because, in today's culture, winning a war involves persuading the people as much as defeating the enemy on the battlefield. Furthermore, it was suggested that a strategy be taken that validates the benefits of peace journalism, demotivates the war media, and concentrates on changing disputes into peaceful resolutions.

CHAPTER SIX

REFERENCES/ BIBLIOGRAPHY

1. "Drone attacks must stop: Nawaz." Pakistan Express Tribune, 9 June 2013. Available at: http://tribune.com.pk/story/560824/drone-attacks-must-stop-nawaz/ (accessed 2 May 2016).

2. Ahmadian, M., & Farahani, E. (2014). A critical discourse analysis of The Los Angeles Times and Tehran Times on the representation of Iran's nuclear program. Theory and Practice in Language Studies, 4(10), 143-156.

3. Ali, A. (2017). Kasmir conflict and South Asian elite press: A framing analysis. Journal of Politics and International Studies , 3(2), 47-62.

4. Amir Shojaei, K. Y. (2013). A CDA approach to the biased interpretation and representation of ideologically conflicting ideas in Western printed media. Journal of Language Teaching and Research, 4(4), 858-868

5. Argenti, P. (1998). Corporate communication, International edition, Irwin McGraw- Hill, Boston.

6. Aslam, R. (2011). Peace journalism: A paradigm shift in traditional media approach. Pacific Journalism Review, 17(1)

7. Bateson, G. (1972). Steps to an ecology of mind: Collected essays in anthropology, psychology, evolution

and epistemology. San Francisco, CA: Chandler

8. Becker, H. (1986b). Photography and Sociology.InDoing things together: Selected papers (pp. 221–272). Evanston, IL: Northwestern University Press.

9. Bernstein, D. (1984) Company image, and reality: a critic of corporate communications, Eastbourne, East Sussex-Great Britain: Holt, Rinehart and Winston Ltd.

10. Boulding, K. E. (1956). The Image: Knowledge in life and Society. Ann Arbor: University of Michigan Press.

11. Brown R. Clausewitz in the age of CNN: Rethinking the military-media relationship. Framing Terrorism: The News Media, the Government, and the Public 2003; 3-23

12. BUCY, Erik. Media Credibility reconsidered: Synergy effects between on-air and online news. Journalism and Mass Communication Quarterly, v. 80, p.247-265, 2003.

13. BuRAKOvSKy, A. (2013), understanding the Determinants of Terrorist Attack Publicity.

14. Cameron, L. (2003). Metaphor in educational discourse. London: Continuum

15. Cappella, J. N., Jamieson, K. L. (1997). Spiral of Cynicism: The Press and the Public Good. Oxford University Press. NY, NY.

16. Chong, D., Druckman, J.N. (2007). Framing Theory. Annual Rev. Polit. Sci. 2007, (10), 103-126.

17. Collier, J., Jr. (1967). Visual anthropology: Photography as a research method.New York: Holt, Rinehart, and Winston.

18. DE gRAAF J., SChMID A. P, (1982), violence as communication, 283p.

19. De Vreese, C. H. "News framing: Theory and typology." Information Design Journal & Document Design 13, no. 1 (2005). 51–62

20. De Vreese, C. H., and H. Boomgaarden. "Valenced news frames and public support for the EU: Linking content analysis and experimental data." Communications: The European Journal of Communication 3 (2003): 261–281.

21. Deutsch, K. W., & Merritt, R. L. (1965). Effects of Events on National and International Images. In: H. C. Kelman (Ed.), International Behaviour A Social-Psychological Analysis New York: Holt, Rinehart, and Winston.

22. Dimitrova, DV and Strömbäck, J. (2012) Election news in Sweden and the United States: A comparative study of sources and media frames. Journalism 13: 604-619.

23. DOWlINg R., E. (1986), Terrorism and the media: A rhetorical genre, Journal of communication,36-1

24. Eissa, M. (2014). Polarized discourse in the news. Procedia-Social and Behavioral Sciences, 134, 70- 91

25. ERDEM, Tülin; SWAIT, Joffre. Brand Credibility and its role in brand choice and consideration. Journal of Consumer Research, v. 31, p.191-199, 2004.

26. Fair, C. C. "Drones, spies, terrorists, and second-class citizenship in Pakistan." Small Wars and Insurgencies 21, no. 3 (2014): 205–235

27. Fair, C. C., Kaltenthaler, K., and Miller, W. "Pakistani Opposition to American Drone Strikes." Political Science Quarterly 129, no. 1 (2014): 1–33.

28. Fair, C. C., Kaltenthaler, K., and Miller, W. "Pakistani Political Communication and Public Opinion on US Drone Attacks." Journal of Strategic Studies (published online January 2015)

29. Fawcett L. Why peace journalism isn't news. Journalism Studies 2002; 3(2): 213-223. https://doi.org/10.1080/14616700220129982

30. Galtung J. Conflict, war and peace: A bird's eye view. Searching For peace: The road to TRANSCEND 2002a; 3- 26. g J. The peace journalism option. Taplow, Conflict & Peace Forums 1998b.

31. Galtung J. High Road, Low Road–Charting the Road for Peace Journalism. Track Two 1998a; 7(4).

32. Galtung J. On the role of the media in worldwide security and peace. Peace and Communication 1986; 249-266

33. GAZIANO, Cecilie; MCGRATH, Kristin. Measuring the Concept of Credibility. Journalism Quarterly, v.. 63 (autumn), p.451-462, 1986.

34. Gilboa, E. (2006). Media in International Conflict. In Oetzel, J. G. & Ting-Toomey, S. The Sage Handbook of Conflict Communication: Integrating Theory, Research, and Practice. (595-626). Thousand Oaks. CA: Sage Publications.

35. Hali, S. M. (2011). Memogate and the NATO attack. The Nation. Published on 11/30/2011.

36. Hallahan, K. (2008). Strategic Framing. International Encyclopedia of Communication, Blackwell

37. Hanitzsch T. Situating peace journalism in journalism studies: A critical appraisal. Conflict and Communication Online 2007; 6(2): 1-9.

38. Haque, J. (2013). PAKISTAN 'S INTERNET LANDSCAPE. Bytes for All, Pakistan

39. Herman ES, Chomsky N. The political economy of the mass media. New York: Pantheon Books 1988.

40. HOEFFLER, Steve; KELLER, Kevin Lane. Building Brand Equity through corporate societal marketing, Journal of Public Policy and Marketing, v. 21, n. 1, p.78-89, 2002.

41. Hoffmann, S. (1968). Perceptions, Reality, and the Franco-American. In: J. C. Farrell & A. P. Smith (Eds.), Image and Reality in World Politics. New York, London: Columbia University Press.

42. Hooghiemstra, R. (2000) Corporate Communication and Impression Management – New Perspectives Why Companies Engage in Corporate Social Reporting. Journal of Business Ethics 27: 55–68, 2000. Kluwer Academic Publishers.

43. Huck, Arthur (1984).Australian Attitudes to China and the Chinese. The Australian Journal of Chinese Affairs, 11, 157-168.

44. Hussain, Jahanzeb. "From Secret to Public: the ISI in Transition." Collateral Damage Magazine, 7 July 2014. Available at: http://collateraldamagemagazine.net/2014/07/07/ from-secret-to-public-the-isi-in-transition/ (accessed 13 Nov 2021).

45. Hussain, Jahanzeb. "From Secret to Public: the ISI in Transition." Collateral Damage Magazine, 7 July 2014. Available at: http://collateraldamagemagazine.net/2014/07/07/ from-secret-to-public-the-isi-in-transition/ (accessed 13 Nov 2021).

46. Hussain, S., & Lynch, J. (2019). Identifying peace-oriented media strategies for deadly conflicts in Pakistan. Information Development, 35(5), 703–713

47. Hussain, S., Siraj, S. A., & Mahmood, T. (2021). Evaluating war and peace potential of Pakistani news media: Advancing a peace journalism model. Information Development, 37(1), 105–121.

48. INFOASAID. "Pakistan: Media and Telecoms Landscape Guide 2012," 2012. Available at: http://www.internews.org/sites/default/files/resources/InfoasAid_Pakistan_ MediaGuide.pdf

(accessed 13 Nov 2021).

49. INFOASAID. "Pakistan: Media and Telecoms Landscape Guide 2012," 2012. Available at: http://www.internews.org/sites/default/files/ resources/InfoasAid_Pakistan_ MediaGuide.pdf (accessed 13 Nov 2021).

50. Iqbal, Z., & Hussain, S. (2018). Indo-Pak wars (1948, 1965, 1971, 1999): Projecting the nationalistic narrative. Journal of Political Studies, 25(1), 139–156.

51. Iyengar, S. & Kinder, D. R. (1987). News that Matters: Television and American Opinions. The University of Chicago Press: Chicago, IL.

52. Iyengar, S. (1991). Is Anyone Responsible? How Television Frames Political Issues. The University of Chicago Press: Chicago, IL.

53. Jalazai, Musa Khan. Sectarianism and politico-religious terrorism in Pakistan. System books, 2000

54. Joanna Slater and Nihan Masih, "Modi vows action after dozens die in deadliest attack in Indian-held Kashmir in 3 decades," The Washington Post, February 15, 2019.

55. Kosslyn, S. M., Ganis, G., and Thompson, W. L. (2003).Mental imagery: against the nihilistic hypothesis.Trends in Cognitive Sciences, 7, 109–11.

56. Krebs, R. "How Dominant Narratives Rise and Fall: Military Conflict, Politics, and the Cold War Consensus." International Organization 69, no. 4 (2015): 1–37

57. Kunczik, Michael (1997). Images of Nations and International Public Relations. Mahweh, N.J.: Lawrence Erlbaum.

58. LeVine, R. A., & Campbell, D. T. (1972).Ethnocentrism: theories of conflict, ethnic attitudes, and group behaviour. New York: Wiley.

59. LeVine, Robert A. (1965). Socialization, Social Structure, and Intersocietal Images. In: H. C. Kelman (Ed.), International Behaviour: A Social-Psychological Analysis: The University of Michigan.

60. Lippmann, W. (1922).Public opinion.New York Free Press.

61. Loyn D. Good journalism or peace journalism. Conflict and Communication Online 2007; 6(2): 1-10

62. Lynch J. Peace journalism and its discontents. Conflict and Communication Online 2007; 6(2): 1-9

63. MAguEN S., A., PAPA AND B.T lITZ. (2008), 'Coping with the threat of terrorism: a review', Anxiety, stress and coping.

64. Mahmood, S. (2002). Pakistan Political Roots & Developments 1947-1999. Oxford: Oxford University Press.

65. Mass Communication Theory (Online). (2017, January 31). Framing Theory. Retrieved from Mass Communication Theory: https://masscommtheory.com/theory-overviews/framing-theory/

66. Meinhof, U. (1998). Language learning in the age of satellite television. Oxford: Oxford University Press.

67. MEYER, Philip. Defining and measuring Credibility of newspapers: Developing an index. Journalism Quarterly, v. 65, p.567-574,1988.

68. Mushtaq, S., &Baig, F. (2015). The Relationship of TV News Channels Consumption with Political Participation, Political Knowledge and Civic Engagement. Asian Social Science, 11(12), 46.

69. Neuman, W. R., Just, M. R., & Crigler, A. N. (1992). Common Knowledge: News and the Construction of Political Meaning. University of Chicago Press. Chicago:

Illinois.

70. Nisbet, M. C. (2009). Communicating Climate Change: Why Frames Matter for Public Engagement, Environment: Science and Policy for Sustainable Development, 51(2), 12-23.

71. NORRIS F. h., FREIDMAN M. J., WATSON P. J., ByRNE C. M., DIAZ E., KANIASTy K. (2002), '6000 disaster victim speak, mental health research

72. Oh, O., Agrawal, M., & Rao, H. R. (2011). Information control and terrorism: Tracking the Mumbai terrorist attack through twitter. Information Systems Frontiers, 13(1), 33–43.

73. Oyedeji the credible brand model: the effects of ideological congruency and customer-based brand equity on news credibility. American Behavioral Scientist, v. 54, n. 2, p. 83-99, 2010.

74. OYEDEJI The relation between the customer-based brand equity of media outlets and their media channel credibility: an exploratory study. The International Journal on Media Management, v. 9, n. 3, p.116-125, 2009. _________ .

75. OYEDEJI, Tayo. The relationship between the media channel credibility and brand equity of media outlets. Journalism Studies Division of International Communication Association (ICA) Conference, Dresden, Germany, 2006.

76. Patel, T. (2005). News coverage and conflict resolution: aid or impediment: a case study of IndiaPakistan conflict over Kashmir. MPhil Thesis, School of Political Science and International Studies, The University of Queensland.

77. Peleg, S. (2006). Peace journalism through the lense of conflict theory: Analysis and practice. Conflict &

Communication Online, 5(2). Retrieved from
http://www.cco.regeneronline.de/2006_2/pdf/
peleg.pdf

78. Perlman, D., &Cozby, P. C. (1981).Social psychology. New York: Holt, Rinehart, and Winston.

79. Podnar, K. (2004). Is it all a question of reputation? The role of branch identity (The case of an oil company), Corporate Reputation Review, 6(4), 376 – 387.

80. Price, V., Tewksbury, D., & Powers, E. (1997). Switching Trains of Thought: The Impact of News Frames on Readers' Cognitive Responses. Communication Research, 24(5), 481-506.

81. Puri, Samir. Pakistan's war on terrorism: Strategies for combating jihadist armed groups since 9/11. Palgrave, 2012.

82. Pylyshyn, Z. W. (2003). Return of the mental image: are there really pictures in the brain? Trends in Cognitive Sciences, 7, 113–8.

83. Qadir, S. (2002). An analysis of the Kargil conflict 1999. The RUSI Journal, 147(2), 24–30.

84. Rabasa, A., Blackwill, R. D., Chalk, P., Cragin, K., & Fair, C. C. (2009). The lessons of Mumbai (Vol. 249). Rand Corporation

85. ROhNER, D., FREy, B. S. (2007), Blood and ink! the common-interest-game between terrorists and the media. Public Choice, 133 (1-2).

86. Scott, W. A. (1965). Psychological and Social Correlates of International Images. In: H. C. Kelman (Ed.), International Behaviour: A Social-Psychological Analysis: The University of Michigan.

87. Shah, D. V., M. D. Watts, D. Domke, and D. P. Fan. "News Framing and Cueing of Issue Regimes: Explaining Clinton's Public Approval In Spite Of Scandal." Public

Opinion Quarterly 66, no. 3 (2002): 339–70.

88. Shah, D. V., M. D. Watts, D. Domke, and D. P. Fan. "News Framing and Cueing of Issue Regimes: Explaining Clinton's Public Approval In Spite Of Scandal." Public Opinion Quarterly 66, no. 3 (2002): 339–70.

89. Shinar D. Media peace discourse: Constraints, concepts and building blocks. Conflict and Communication Online 2004; 3(1-2).

90. Shinar D. Reflections on media war coverage: Dissonance, dilemmas, and the need for improvement. Conflict & Communication 2013; 12(2).

91. Shoemaker, P. J., & Reese, S. D. (1996). MEDIATING THE MESSAGE. Longman Publishers USA.

92. Siddiqa, Ayesha. "Pakistan's Counterterrorism Strategy: Separating Friends from Enemies. (May 7 ,2015)" Council on Foreign Relations.

93. SIlvER, R. C., hOlMAN, E. A., ANDERSEN, J. P., POulIN, M., MCINTOSh, D. N., & gIlRIvAS, v. (2013), Mental and Physical-health Effects of Acute Exposure to Media Images of the September 11 , 2001 , Attacks and the Iraq War.

94. Singh, Ritika. "Lawfare Podcast Episode #20: Daniel Markey on US-Pakistan Terrorism Cooperation and Pakistan's Extremist Groups." 27 September 2012. Available at: http://www.lawfareblog.com/2012/09/daniel-markey-on-u-s-pakistan-terrorismcooperation-and-pakistans-extremist-groups (accessed 13 Nov 2021).

95. Singh, Ritika. "Lawfare Podcast Episode #20: Daniel Markey on US-Pakistan Terrorism Cooperation and Pakistan's Extremist Groups." 27 September 2012. Available at: http://www.lawfareblog.com/2012/09/daniel-markey-on-u-s-pakistan-terrorismcooperation-

and-pakistans-extremist-groups (accessed 13 Nov 2021).

96. Social Policy and Development Centre. "Social Development in Pakistan: Annual Review 2012–13." 2014. Available at: http://www.spdc.org.pk/ Publication_detail. aspx?sysID=762 (accessed 13 Nov 2021).

97. Social Policy and Development Centre. "Social Development in Pakistan: Annual Review 2012–13." 2014. Available at: http://www.spdc.org.pk/ Publication_detail. aspx?sysID=762 (accessed 13 Nov 2021).

98. Social Policy and Development Centre. "Social Development in Pakistan: Annual Review 2011–12." 2012. Available at: www.spdc.org.pk/Publications/ Annual%20Reviews/ AR%,2011.pdf (accessed 13 Nov 2021).

99. Spiegel Online. (2011). US-Kongress will Millionen-Hilfe für Pakistan einfrieren. Published on 12/13/2011.

100. Tahir, M. (2013). A critical discourse analysis of religious othering of Muslims in the Washington Post. Middle-East Journal of Scientific Research, 14(6), 744-753

101. Tewksbury, D. & Scheufele, D.A. (2008). News framing theory and research. In J. Bryant & M.B. Oliver (Eds.). Advance in theory and research (3rd ed., 17-33), New York, USA: Routledge.

102. U.S. Department of Defense. (2011). DoD News Briefing with Brig. Gen. Clarke via Teleconference from Hurlburt Field, Fla. Published 12/22/2011. http://archive.defense.gov/Transcripts/ Transcript.aspx?TranscriptID=4952. Accessed on 8/1/

2017.

103. UNESCO. (2014). "Country Profiles – Pakistan (2014)." 2014. Available at: www.uis.unesco. org/DataCentre/Pages/country-profile.aspx?code=PAK®ioncode=40535 (accessed 13 Nov 2021)

104. UNESCO. (2014). "Country Profiles – Pakistan (2014)." 2014. Available at: www.uis.unesco. org/DataCentre/Pages/country-profile.aspx?code=PAK®ioncode=40535 (accessed 13 Nov 2021)

105. UNESCO. (2014). "Country Profiles – Pakistan (2014)." 2014. Available at: www.uis.unesco. org/DataCentre/Pages/country-profile.aspx?code=PAK®ioncode=40535 (13 Nov 2021)

106. UNOCHA. "Pakistan: Getting through winter in the north-west." 1 February 2014. Available at: http://www.unocha.org/pakistan/top-stories/pakistan-getting-through-winternorth-west (accessed 13 Nov 2021).

107. UNOCHA. "Pakistan: Getting through winter in the north-west." 1 February 2014. Available at: http://www.unocha.org/pakistan/top-stories/pakistan-getting-through-winternorth-west (accessed 13 Nov 2021).

108. US Department of State, Bureau of Democracy, Human Rights and Labor. "Country Reports on Human Rights Practices for 2014: Pakistan." 2014. Available at: http://www. state.gov/documents/organization/236860.pdf (accessed 13 Nov, 2021).

109. Van Ham, P. (2002). Branding territory. Inside the wonderful worlds of PR and IR theory. Millennium-

Journal of International Studies, 31(2), 249-269.

110. Wang, J. (2008). The power and limits of branding in national image communication in global society. International Political Communication,14(2), 9-24.

111. White, Margaret (1999). Improving Image Literacy about China: a Study of Process Shaping Australian Perceptions. Melbourne studies in education, 40(1), 57-76.

112. Whyte K. The Uncrowned King: The Sensational Rise of William Randolph Hearst: Vintage Canada 2009.

113. Yusuf, Huma. "Conspiracy Fever: the US, Pakistan and its Media." Survival 53, no. 4 (2011): 95–118.